The

This Book
Belongs to:

Janet Toye

Morning Glory-by Catherine Hamilton

John Macquarrie

The Mediators

Nine Stars in the Human Sky

SCM PRESS LTD

0 334 02621 0

First published 1995
by SCM Press Ltd
9–17 St Albans Place, London N1 0NX

Typeset at The Spartan Press Ltd,
Lymington, Hants
Printed in Finland by
Werner Söderström Oy

Contents

Contents

Preface

When I was studying theology at the University of Glasgow more than fifty years ago, the Faculty of Divinity there was operating a very enlightened policy (for that time) in the matter of non-Christian religions. Two optional courses were offered to final-year students, one in Buddhism and one in Islam. Both were taught by highly qualified teachers. The course in Buddhism was taught by Professor A.J. Gossip, one of the very few people in Britain with a knowledge of the Pali language, in which are written the scriptures of the Theravada canon; while the course in Islam was presented by Dr James Robson, who had lived for many years in Arabia and who later became Professor of Arabic in the University of Manchester. These studies confirmed something which I already believed – that there are genuine revelations of God outside of the Judaeo-Christian tradition, and that there is much to be learned from these non-biblical revelations.

I have said that the policy at Glasgow was enlightened in those rather far-off days, but I have lived long enough to see a dramatic change. The study of non-Christian religions which was then considered an optional extra in Christian faculties of theology has now moved much closer to the centre. This present book is offered, primarily to Western and Christian readers, as a way into the current dialogue among the great religions of the world.

But that subject is so vast and demanding that I have limited the area covered to studies of the outstanding spiritual geniuses, probably less than a dozen, whose visions of God in relation to the human situation have been, and still are, among the most powerful factors shaping the lives of billions of human beings on this planet, not only in the narrowly religious sphere, but in morals, politics, culture, virtually everything that constitutes human existence.

My debts to many people are too numerous to be listed in detail: to the early teachers mentioned above, to many personal contacts made with students in my classes and with scholars met on lecture trips to the East, and to the many writers and translators who have opened up for us Westerners the wisdom of the East. These debts are acknowledged in the notes to the several chapters.

Oxford, June 1995   John Macquarrie

In the new Europe, as elsewhere, there is a new form of spiritual journey, new for Christianity and for all the traditions in this late twentieth century. The new search is likely to become that of more and more religious persons; stay faithful to your own tradition; go more and more deeply into its particularities; defend and clarify its identity. At the same time, wander Ulysses-like, willingly, even eagerly, among other great traditions and ways; try to learn something of their beauty and truth; concentrate on their otherness and difference as the new route to communicality.

(David Tracy, *On Naming the Present*,
SCM Press and Orbis Books 1995, p. 137)

Introduction

Among those who are interested in theology and religious studies, there is at the present time no more interesting topic than that of the relations of the great religions of the world. In the past, these relations were often characterized by indifference or even hostility, but today there is a widespread desire for dialogue and understanding. To a large extent, inter-religious dialogue has been forced upon us by changes that have already taken place in society. In Maurice Wiles' words, such dialogue is 'inescapable for the theologian, however limited his or her personal experience of it, since the close co-existence of different faith communities in our one world – indeed for very many people the co-existence of such communities in the immediate locality or institution in which they live or work – is a distinctive feature of our experience'.[1]

No doubt there had always been some dialogue that went beyond mere polemic. As early as the middle of the second century, the Christian philosopher and theologian, Justin the Martyr, wrote his *Dialogue with Trypho a Jew*. This work for the most part was an attempt to show the superiority of Christianity over Judaism, but there were some moments of genuine dialogue in it. In the sixteenth and seventeenth centuries, when thitherto unknown parts of the world were being opened up by explorers from the West, Christian theologians were debating whether the inhabitants of those areas who had never heard of Christ might nevertheless be saved by an 'implicit' faith. By the eighteenth century, Jesuits were reporting on the highly rational religion of the Chinese, and there was something of a cult of everything Chinese among Western peoples. The nineteenth century saw the translation of many classic religious texts into European languages and this led to an upsurge of sympathetic understanding. In 1893 in Chicago there took place a Parliament of Religions and it may have seemed that dialogue was fully launched.

But the first half of the twentieth century brought a reaction. The theology of Karl Barth opposed to the notion of religion, understood as the human quest for God, the notion of revelation, and this was claimed to have come exclusively through Christ. The Barthian view was reinforced by the teaching of Hendrik Kraemer who applied it to the mission situation and, holding that the Christian revelation is *sui generis* and incompatible with other so-called 'revelations', drew the conclusion that, for Christians, co-operation with non-Christian faiths is virtually a betrayal of their own faith. Unfortunately, Barth and Kraemer had an enormous influence on the World Council of Churches, and for many years that body shunned anything that might savour of 'syncretism'.

In 1964 I published an article entitled 'Christianity and Other Faiths' in the *Union Seminary Quarterly Review*.[2] I continue to hold the views I expressed then. To put these views in a sentence, I believe that, however difficult it may be, we should hold to our own traditions and yet respect and even learn from the traditions of others. I drew the conclusion that there should be an end to proselytizing but that equally there should be no syncretism of the kind typified by the Baha'i movement. The article aroused a good deal of discussion, and in the next issue of the *Review* there were five replies from well-known theologians. Paul Tillich and Roger Shinn (both of Union Seminary) together with Seymour Siegel (Jewish Theological Seminary) were in broad agreement with what I had written; J.R. Chandran (United Theological Seminary, Bangalore) and Paul Lehmann (a colleague and good friend at Union) strongly disagreed. Professor Chandran's main point was that the position I had taken may come rather easily to one living and teaching in the West, but things seem very different to a member of the small Christian minority in countries such as India and Japan. Paul Lehmann forthrightly declared that my article was 'a perfect formula for modern Hinduism' but not for Christianity, and claimed that one can maintain the uniqueness and exclusiveness of Christian faith without falling into arrogance. I acknowledge that both of these objections have some force, but not enough, I think, to overturn the arguments I had put forward. But perhaps to combine a claim to uniqueness with an avoidance of arrogance is no more difficult than my recommendation of commitment and openness.

Now, more than thirty years later, the discussion has moved on again, the objections to dialogue seem to have fallen silent even in the

World Council of Churches, and relations with the non-Christian religions seem to have moved to the top of the Christian theological agenda. What are the reasons for this change?

One reason has already been given above – the social changes that have brought adherents of different religious groups into close proximity with one another. Unfortunately, in our compact world of today, there has been a disquieting increase of nationalism, tribalism and fundamentalism, all posing a grave threat for the future. The religions are under pressure to draw together for the sake of humanity. But not only secular pressures are at work. Vatican II must be recognized as a landmark in the search for peace and co-operation among the religions. The Council declared:

> In our times, when every day men are being drawn closer together and the ties between various peoples are being multiplied, the church is giving deeper study to her relationship with non-Christian religions. In her task of fostering unity and love among men, and even among nations, she gives primary consideration in this document to what human beings have in common and to what promotes fellowship among them.[3]

This was the opening sentence of a document entitled 'Declaration on the Relationship of the church to Non-Christian Religions'. The document goes on to speak in conciliatory terms not only of the general religious quest of the human race but of specific religions including Hinduism, Buddhism, Islam and Judaism. The affirmative aims of the Catholic Church toward other religions are summed up in the following sentences: 'The Catholic Church rejects nothing which is true and holy in these religions. She looks with sincere respect upon those ways of conduct and of life, those rules and teachings which, though differing in many particulars from what she holds and sets forth, nevertheless often reflect a ray of that truth which enlightens all men.'[4]

Of necessity the declaration of the Council was stated in very general terms, but individual Catholic theologians have, in the spirit of the Vatican declaration, produced more detailed and specific proposals for dialogue and collaboration among the religions. One of the earliest responses to the Council's declaration, but still one of the best, was the book of Heinz Robert Schlette, *Towards a Theology of Religions*. In it he argued that the (non-Christian) religions are willed by God and are ways of salvation. Karl Rahner also interested himself in the question of the religions, and his teaching that the good Buddhist or Muslim may be deemed an 'anonymous Christian' is very well-known. Surely, however, it is much too patronizing a view and overlooks the differences among the religions. More recently, Hans Küng has turned to these problems, and particularly to reconciliation among the so-called 'Abrahamic' religions, Judaism, Christianity and Islam. He has summed up his teaching in a formula or slogan appearing in several of his books: 'No peace among the nations without peace among the religions. No peace among the religions without dialogue among the religions. No dialogue among the religions without investigation of the foundations of the religions.'[5] The last of Küng's three sentences seems to give very special importance to historical investigation. No doubt this is of importance, but we must be careful not to think that it would be sufficient in itself.

Alongside these Catholic writers, one must set the work of Protestant scholars whose studies have done much to promote better understanding and so better friendship among the religions. One may mention John Hick, Ninian Smart and Wilfred Cantwell Smith as among the best-known. Yet even in mentioning these names, a painful embarrassment arises. The names I have cited are only a tiny fraction of the vast number engaged in the study of religions. Worse still, the handful mentioned are all Western and presumably Christian. But it takes two at least to make a dialogue. We have to be aware of all the contributions that have come from non-Christian and non-Western sources. India has produced many scholars, of whom the best-known in recent times was Sarvepalli Radhakrishnan, professor in Oxford for many years and eventually president of his country. Japan has sent out ambassadors for Buddhism, such as D. Suzuki, M. Abe and Y. Takeuchi, all of them writers whose works are well-known in the West. One could add names from China and from the Islamic countries, while resident in the West there have been many Jewish scholars, and some of them – Cohen, Buber, Rosenzweig, Heschel, to name only a few – have had quite a considerable influence on Christian theology.

But just to mention these points is to draw attention to the overwhelming difficulties that lie in the way of any *rapprochement* among the religions. The sheer vastness of the field is the first obvious discouragement. To get to know any one religion thoroughly is a lifetime's study. I have myself spent over fifty years studying and teaching Christianity, and there are still innumerable things I do not know about it. Before I was allowed to begin these studies, I had to pass examinations in Latin, Greek and Hebrew. If I wished to study Buddhism, let us say, then if I were going to do so with proper respect, treating it as seriously as Christianity, I would have to begin by learning the Pali language, probably also Chinese and Japanese, then read a vast literature and learn twenty-five centuries of the history of Buddhism and the backgrounds against which it has developed. But even that amount of study (if it were possible) would give only a theoretical knowledge. I would have to live for a longish period of time in a Buddhist environment, perhaps in a monastery, in order to come to grips with Buddhism in an existential way, for a religion is a way of living, not just a doctrine about living. So if one were to apply oneself with equal seriousness to several religions, one would need to have several lifetimes at one's disposal.[6]

Of course, the situation envisaged in the preceding paragraph makes impossible demands, and no individual human being could fulfil them. All that is possible is to attain *some* understanding of the other faith, *some* competence in moving about among its ideas and in entering into its aspirations. After all, people do write very useful and illuminating books on the religions of the world, though they cannot know them all equally well or treat them all in full detail. A vast amount of study must lie behind such standard works as A.C. Bouquet's *Comparative Religion* and R.N. Smart's *The Religious Experience of Mankind* and they certainly offer enough to allow a dialogue to get started and a relationship of respect to develop.

If the vastness of the material is the first discouragement in any approach to the study of religions, the next one is perhaps even more serious. It is the fact, totally inescapable, that each of us sees this material from a particular point of view. We have already taken a stance, so that we see things from a particular angle, and because of this, there may be many things that we can never see properly. The natural scientist used to cultivate what was called a 'value-free' approach to his subject-matter, that is to say, he tried to exclude from consideration all judgments of, say, right and wrong or beautiful and ugly. Such qualities were supposed to be 'subjective' and the aim was to study the material in a purely 'objective' way. Nowadays even some natural scientists question whether a value-free approach is possible and as far as the human sciences are concerned, the ideal of a value-free knowledge has been virtually abandoned. There is always a personal dimension in knowledge and naturally it is stronger in the knowledge of human affairs.

The student of religion comes to the subject-matter not with a mind that is a *tabula rasa*, but as a person already holding certain religious (or possibly irreligious) convictions. Now this need not of itself prevent an understanding of the subject-matter of the study; on the contrary, it might be argued that only someone who had *some* religious experience could really understand what *any* religion is about. Otherwise it could hardly be anything but a closed book. The danger is that one's presuppositions may be allowed to become so dominant that they do prevent any openness toward the subject-matter, and this once again remains a closed book. Fortunately, we can all to some extent criticize our own presuppositions and prevent them from degenerating into a fanatical obsession. We can make an effort toward sympathizing with the different religion, we can look for resemblances and thus points of agreement with our own religious beliefs, and we can recognize differences and perhaps ask ourselves whether they can be bridged. Something like the situation described would seem to be the *sine qua non* for any dialogue whatsoever. If two would-be participants in dialogue believe they have nothing in common, the dialogue will never begin; but if they are in total agreement, dialogue is no longer necessary. In the dialogue of the religions, the participants bring with them strong convictions and often what confronts them seems utterly strange and unintelligible. But if they find a place to begin, they will often be surprised to find how naturally the dialogue moves along, and although quite major differences may remain, each has learned from the other to see things somewhat differently. Speaking from a Christian point of view, Schlette remarks, 'Christianity affects other religions and is in turn perfected by them.'[7] I think I would prefer to say, 'affected' rather than 'perfected'.

The present book is meant to be a small contribution to the dialogue of the religions. It is written from a Christian point of view, but it is written not only with the intention of being open to other religions but with the hope and expectation of learning from these other traditions so that one's own tradition may be purified and enriched through the exchanges. But I am not intending to write on the various religions as such. I have chosen a more modest task, that of writing on the handful of outstanding human beings who have inspired the great world religions. I say 'inspired' rather than 'founded', for whatever new insights they brought, I think they all built on foundations that had been laid long before.

There are certain ideas or structures that seem to recur in all the great religions. The most obvious of these is a conception of God, or, to use a somewhat vague term which I have found convenient, of Holy Being. But in most of these religions is also to be found a human figure who has brought that conception of God to the people. In some cases it may be appropriate to speak of 'revelation', in others, that may be less appropriate. In some cases, the human figure may be believed to embody the God, in other cases he is a teacher with privileged knowledge. In every case, however, he – I suppose it might have been 'she' but as a fact of history, one must write 'he' – has as it were had an encounter with God which he then passes on to the people. The poet Hölderlin assigns a very similar function to the poet and expresses it in a vivid manner, reminding us that the office of bringing God to man is one of danger as well as privilege:

> Yet it behoves us, under the storms of God,
> Ye poets! with uncovered head to stand,
> With our own hand to grasp the Father's lightning-flash
> And to pass on, wrapped in words,
> The divine gift to the people.[8]

Of course, in the days when the great geniuses of religion were active, the offices of poet and prophet had not yet been separated. The office of priest is not far distant, but the priest represents the people to God as well as bringing God to the people.

I have called these human figures of the great religions 'mediators'. This seemed to me to be the most inclusive term available. In an earlier book, I used the expression 'saviour figures' and wrote about 'Jesus Christ and the Saviour Figures'.[9] The word 'saviour' is frequently used of Jesus Christ, but would hardly be appropriate to Confucius. Again, while the Buddha of the Mahayana type of Buddhism appears as a saviour, the word could hardly be used of the Buddha of Theravada (so-called Hinayana) Buddhism. Similar remarks apply to the word 'redeemer', which seems to imply a doctrine of atonement. The word 'prophet' is also limited in its application. The word received its connotations in the Hebrew scriptures and Moses is the type of the prophet; Mohammad is often called a 'prophet', but opinions are divided about the applicability of the words to Jesus and it is doubtful if it could be used outside of the

Abrahamic religions. So when I speak of the 'mediators' and even use the title *The Mediators* for the book, I am including several types of religious leader under the expression.

Actually the term 'mediators' was used by Schleiermacher, often called the founder of modern theology, in his famous *Speeches on Religion to its Cultured Despisers*. In the last of his speeches, Schleiermacher tells us that Jesus is not the only mediator, and he then uses the word in the plural to designate the human figures who have the foremost place in other religions though he does not specify them by name. But he does speak in this context of God, in face of the increasing alienation of his creation, 'scattering points here and there over the whole that are at once finite and infinite, human and divine.'[10]

These words of Schleiermacher about scattering points over the universe were in my mind when I chose as the subtitle of the book the words, 'Nine Stars in the Human Sky'. The human sky is often dull and sometimes very dark, but through all the centuries of struggle, the religions have been a source of hope and encouragement. Their teaching has been that this universe of ours is not a sorry accident but has some end or purpose which makes even its sufferings worthwhile. The message of the great religions is that the ultimate reality is God, that there is a spiritual power stronger than any physical force, that God will not abandon his creation but will bring salvation, even if we do not know how he will do that or even what that salvation will be. We can have no more than glimpses and the religions supply these glimpses. 'The fact of religious vision, and its history of persistent expansion, is our one ground for optimism', wrote Whitehead many years ago. I do not think that vision is an illusion, though even if it were, its practical benefits in keeping alive hope and in fostering peace and justice would perhaps be sufficient justification. It has brought the light of hope, and it is hard to believe that this hope could have captivated human hearts and minds if there were not also with it the light of truth.[11]

Now that light has come to us through the mediators, those scattered points in space and time which I have likened to stars in the human sky. We use the word 'star' nowadays not only for the heavenly bodies, but for human beings, both men and women, who shine in sport or entertainment and whose achievements in these fields bring pleasure to their fellows. But perhaps the greatest stars are the mediators of the religious reality, who have brought to us not merely fleeting pleasures but solid joys that enrich human life at the deepest levels.

Why have I talked of *nine* stars? The number itself has no significance. It might have been greater or it might have been smaller. I think, however, that the number of really outstanding creative spiritual geniuses who have deeply affected the lives of millions is probably less than a dozen, an incredibly small fraction out of the billions of human beings. But that seems to be nature's way at all levels. For instance, out of the billions of stars in the universe, there seem to be only a very small number that have planets that could bring forth creatures like ourselves. But to come back to the question, 'Why nine?', let me say this was no arbitrary choice but one that seems to be determined by the history of religion. Karl Jaspers wrote about an 'axial age' in the history of the human race. He dated it roughly from 800 to 200 BCE, and claimed that this axis or turning-point was 'the point most overwhelmingly fruitful in fashioning humanity'.[12] This period, he claims, marked the maturing of man as a spiritual and personal being, and it was a time when all over the globe there appeared outstanding moral and spiritual leaders. These included the Hebrew prophets, the philosophers of Greece, the great thinkers of China, Buddha and others in India . . . The list could be expanded. Were there, for instance, comparable figures in Africa or in the Americas, though we know nothing about them because there were no records at that time in those regions? Nor have any world religions come out of these regions which might have preserved memories of their past. Perhaps we could expand Jaspers' axial age in time, even though we cannot expand the catchment area in space. For instance, he mentions the Hebrew prophets, and presumably he has in mind Amos, Hosea, Isaiah, Jeremiah, Ezekiel and others who did work during the axial period. But the greatest figure in Hebrew religion, Moses, is excluded because he must have lived about five hundred years before the period began. Jaspers' cut-off point, 200 BCE, has the further disadvantage of excluding Jesus and Muhammad, though their followers constitute the two most numerous religious bodies in the world today. So we still have not justified the figure of nine.

Near the beginning of this introduction, I mentioned briefly the Parliament of religions which met in Chicago in 1893. This Parliament was part of the celebrations connected with the 500th anniversary of Columbus' discovery of America, understood as a major step in the formation of a worldwide human community. At the beginning of the session of the Parliament, a great bell was rung ten times. This was because ten world faiths were represented. But actually three of the ten were Christian, for Roman Catholicism, Eastern Orthodoxy and Protestantism were counted as separate religions! These three religions all look to one mediator, Jesus Christ. Japanese Shintoism was represented, but there is no one figure who represents it as a 'mediator' in the sense in which we are using the word. On the other hand, Socrates as a moral teacher of the axial age has a good claim to be counted as a mediator, and though he did not found a religion, he may be taken to represent that Greek strain which combined with the Hebrew heritage so as to produce the specifically Christian ethos. So putting them in chronological order, our nine stars turn out to be Moses, Zoroaster, Lao-zu,[13] Buddha, Confucius, Socrates, Krishna, Jesus, Muhammad.

It may be useful at this point to make a few general comments on these nine figures. The first point is that they are figures of *history*. To say that is also to say that they were human beings. It may seem strange to begin writing about people with an assertion that they did in fact exist! I think, however, that this is an important point when one considers the theological significance of any of these mediators. Of course, some of them lived a very long time ago and even the most recent, Muhammad, was born more than 1400 years ago. Details about them are scarce or, in some cases, virtually non-existent. But we have before us today living communities and living traditions and the most natural way to explain them is to accept their own confession that they are who they are because of Muhammad, or whoever it is to whom they look back.

The problem is not just lack of historical information. We know very little about many figures of antiquity, but normally we do not question the fact that they existed. The problem with the mediators is that just because of the impact which they made, they became the subjects of all kinds of impossible *legends*. Actually, similar legends often grew up about very different mediators, and it is unlikely that stories told about one were transferred to others. It is more likely that these legends arose independently, and the fact that similar legends attach to quite different persons would seem to be due to the expectations of their followers, and these expectations had a universal currency in the religious mind of antiquity. Thus stories of a miraculous birth attach to several of our mediators, but it seems quite clear that in fact nothing was known about the actual birth, and the story was invented because the disciples of the mediator believed that this is how it ought to have been. Another story that we find in several cases is that a wicked ruler tried to have the child put to death. Still another is that at the end of the mediator's life, he ascended into heaven. We shall see examples of this mythological tendency as we study the various mediators, but none of these mediators, I think, is wholly dissolved into legend.

Another point about the mediators is that all of them are believed to have had a *special relation* to God or to Holy Being. They were not just mouthpieces relaying a message but themselves had some share in the holiness of God. They were holy men or men of God, and some of them have actually been worshipped. All have at least been venerated by their followers, but I doubt if any (with the possible exception of Krishna) have actually been identified with God.

The most intimate union between God and the mediator is probably expressed in the idea of *incarnation* and this is a very complex idea. It has been discussed in great detail especially in Christian theology. This is not the place to discuss the matter in detail, but Christ is not simply identified with God. In Indian religion, Krishna is an incarnation (strictly speaking, an *avatar* or descent) of the high god Vishnu but here Krishna has tended to absorb Vishnu and to become himself the high god. The kind of incarnation visualized in Krishnaism would perhaps correspond to Apollinarianism in Christianity, for in Hinduism the relation of soul to body is a fairly 'loose' one – the soul can migrate from one body to another. In this way of thinking, Vishnu animates the body of Krishna, but does not assume Krishna's total humanity.

Some writers have claimed that Christianity's doctrine of the Incarnation of the Word in Jesus Christ rules out any genuine dialogue with other faiths. This would be true only if the doctrine were interpreted in the exclusive sense associated with Barth and Kraemer, and criticized above. But it certainly need not be interpreted in that way, and many Christians would allow that the Word or Logos is not confined to Jesus Christ. Then incarnation facilitates dialogue, for other religions than Christianity have similar teachings (we have just seen an example in the incarnationist teaching about Krishna) and can readily discuss what incarnation might mean. I remember an interesting illustration of this, from an occasion when I was leading a seminar on the person of Jesus Christ in Jabalpur

(Central India). A member of the group, who was of high brahmin background, interjected one day when I was talking on these matters, 'In India, Christology is possible only as Krishnology', an assertion that needs to be pondered.

A third point that calls to be mentioned concerning the mediators is that each of them has gathered about himself *a body of scripture*. Few of them wrote anything themselves, but disciples recorded some of their teaching and sometimes recorded also events in their careers. The records have to be critically examined, though unfortunately they are sometimes treated as if they were themselves infallible. But the mediators were living persons and cannot be reduced to books. Someone made a good point about Jesus: he wrote only in the sand, and nobody knows what he wrote.[14] What would he have made of the Christian literalist or fundamentalist who insists that every word in the New Testament is inspired by the Holy Spirit?

It is time for us now to turn to the mediators and to consider them one by one, taking them in chronological order. Perhaps it is hardly necessary for me to say that there will be no attempt to show that any one of them is superior to the others. I think that what has already been said in this introduction has shown the impossibility of any such judgment. No human being – and certainly not the present writer – has the exhaustive knowledge of the several mediators or the requisite criteria for making such a judgment. Neither does he or she have the detached situation that would enable a purely objective view of the question. Only God, I suppose, could make such a judgment. But if the judgment of superiority is impossible, one must say the same about the judgment of the so-called liberal who declares that these mediators are all of equal stature and authority. And the reasons for ruling out the 'liberal' view are exactly the same – the person who makes it has neither the knowledge nor the criteria nor the Olympian detachment required.

I have acknowledged that I write myself as a Christian theologian, I do so because this is the channel of mediation through which the truth of God has impinged on me. I do not deny for a moment that the truth of God has reached others through other channels – indeed, I hope and pray that it has. So while I have a special attachment to one mediator, I have respect for them all and have tried to give a fair presentation of each.

Moses

(Thirteenth Century BCE)

We think first of all of Moses, the earliest of the nine mediators who will be considered in this book. The exact dates of his birth and death are unknown, but modern research places him with some confidence in the thirteenth century BCE. As we shall see, the exodus of some Hebrew tribes from Egypt probably occurred about the year 1250, and Moses was the leading spirit in that episode. Although this takes us back more than 3000 years, I do not think that there are many historians who would doubt the historicity of the persons and events which will be described. One historian of Israel writes, 'It is quite impossible to deny either the fact of the exodus or the historicity of Moses.'[1] Of course, I am not saying that all the details about Moses that have come down to us are true. Some of these are obviously legendary, and resemble legends that have been told about other mediators. But the general outlines of Moses' career and teaching are clear enough.

Moses, as has been mentioned, became the leader of a group of Hebrew tribes and these at a later time became the people of Israel. Already in the fifteenth century BCE there are references to people called Habiru. The people known by this name do not seem to have been a distinct ethnic group. They were nomads, speaking a Semitic language and going from place to place to undertake what work might be available, ranging from hard manual labour to serving as mercenaries in armies. We hear of them in the famous Tell el-Amarna letters[2] when they were apparently causing trouble to the Egyptian garrisons in the occupied territories of Syria. Some of these people had entered Egypt and settled in the northern part of the country. They may have come during the period when Egypt was ruled by the Hyksos kings, a foreign dynasty of Asian origin, which may well have encouraged Semitic kinsmen to come into Egypt. These migrants appear to have flourished, but when a native dynasty regained control of the country, the position of the migrants became insecure. These migrants had retained traditions of earlier leaders, especially Joseph, who had brought them into Egypt and had enjoyed the favour of the Egyptian rulers. But 'now there arose a new king of Egypt who did not know Joseph'.[3] This new Pharaoh (possibly Sethos I, who reigned from 1293–1279) was understandably alarmed by the growth of the immigrant population, and he imposed on them a kind of *corvée* or system of forced labour which they regarded as virtual slavery. But according to the Hebrew scriptures, 'the more they were oppressed, the more they multiplied', and the king resorted to more severe measures. What happened at this point sounds more like the legendary 'wicked king' *motif* familiar in some of these stories of mediators than like a record of actual fact. The king gave orders that all male children of the Hebrews should be thrown into the Nile. It was under these circumstances that Moses was born, the child of an enslaved Hebrew couple.

The legend goes on to tell that the parents kept the child secretly for three months, but when he could no longer be hidden the mother made a basket or 'ark' of bulrushes, treated it with pitch to make it waterproof, and then placed it with the child in it among the reeds at the river's edge. The daughter of Pharaoh came down to bathe in the river, saw the basket and sent one of her maids to fetch it. When the basket was brought, the child naturally enough was crying, and Pharaoh's daughter was overcome with pity. So she arranged for Moses to be brought up in the royal court, and it even came about that the Hebrew woman hired to look after the child was none other than Moses' own mother! So Moses had, if not exactly a miraculous birth, at least a very fortunate beginning to his career.

It is possible that the story is not only told as befitting one who was to become a great hero of his people, but also as an explanation of Moses' name. It is generally agreed that the name Moses (in Hebrew, Mosheh) is an Egyptian name. This is accounted for in the legend by the statement that the name was given to the child by Pharaoh's daughter, who adopted him as her son. But one can hardly accept the further explanation given in the Bible that seeks to derive the name from a Hebrew verb, since it is hardly likely that the princess would want her adopted son to be known by a name derived from the slave language, even if she had any acquaintance with that language. So the question arises, 'Was Moses really an Egyptian?' It is at least conceivable that he was an Egyptian, possibly a high-ranking Egyptian, who took pity on the Hebrew slaves and became their champion. The writers of the Hebrew scriptures would not have entertained the possibility that Moses could have been anything other than a good Hebrew, but the possibility that he was Egyptian cannot be ruled out. There is a further point here. Although the name Moses appears to be Egyptian, it was used as only part of a name, as for instance in the name Thutmose, borne by several Egyptian kings, and meaning 'son of the (deity) Thoth'. It has been speculated that Moses' name had originally an earlier part, probably the name of an Egyptian god. But nobody knows what this earlier part of the name may have been. Presumably it was dropped after Moses had come out against the Egyptian state and had declared himself a worshipper of Yahweh.

The traditional story of Moses goes on to tell us of a decisive incident that occurred when he was a young man. He went out on a kind of tour of inspection of the Hebrews. He saw them engaged in hard labour, and he also saw one of them being beaten by an Egyptian guard. In a burst of indignation, he killed the Egyptian and concealed his body in the sand. Going out again next day, he saw two Hebrews struggling together, and rebuked them. One of them replied with a question that has become part of the English language: 'Who made you a ruler and a judge over us?' Realizing that it had become known that he had killed the Egyptian, Moses decided to go into hiding. So he fled to Midian, an area east of the Gulf of Aqaba. This flight ends the first phase of Moses' life, and leaves him estranged from the Egyptian authorities, and probably in danger of his life if he should fall into their hands.

Moses seems to have prospered in Midian, and there he married a daughter of the priest of the country. It must have been during this period that his religious thinking developed. His life was that of a shepherd, and there was plenty of time for thought as he followed his flock through the far from fertile countryside. It is easy to believe that the stillness of the landscape and the vastness of the sky in that region would be profoundly impressive for anyone with a religious or, even more, a mystical temperament. Meanwhile, some news of political developments filtered through to Midian. The position of the Hebrews had not improved but seemed to be worsening. King Sethos had died, but his successor, Rameses II, was no less of a tyrant. Rameses was a teenager when he ascended the throne, and he reigned through most of the thirteenth century, from 1279 to 1213. He was an ambitious builder, and seems to have used the Hebrew slaves to erect his extravagent structures. Moses was made aware of what was going on. So in Moses there was in this formative period an interesting and perhaps very unusual confluence of the contemplative and the practical: the contemplative, in so far as his quiet life of shepherding on the plains encouraged thought about God and the meaning of human life; practical, in so far as his own years of exile and the news of the sufferings of his people back in Egypt were an incentive to find a way of acting for the amelioration of their situation.

The climax of this period in Moses' career was a religious experience which must surely rank as one of the most significant in the entire history of religion. He was with his flock in the wilderness, not far from 'Horeb, the mountain of God', a mountain of which we shall be hearing later. His eye was caught by a shining bush, which appeared to be on fire and yet was not being consumed. Perhaps it was simply that the leaves of that bush were catching the sun's rays in such a way that it stood out sharply in the somewhat dreary landscape. As Moses approached it, he was overcome with an overwhelming sense of the holiness of the place and the presence of God there. The theophany or revelation of God that came to him on that occasion was an inner experience that presumably only Moses himself knew at first hand. The experience was, of course, evoked by things and events that were publicly observable: by the bush that burned, by the environment of land and sky, by the human situation over there in Egypt, of which he had news and which he could visualize in imagination. These things and events were like the outward symbols of a sacrament, embodying and effecting the inward experience. But when someone has an experience of that order, then one tries to put it into words, both to deepen one's own understanding of it and to share it with other people. We do not have direct access to what was going on in Moses' inner experience, but we have the words in which Moses and his interpreters have sought to express and communicate his experience. If we look carefully at these words, we can, I believe, discern a definite structure in the experience, and we may then be on the lookout for similar structures in the experiences of other mediators.

What structure then is it possible to discern? First we hear of a voice which directly addresses Moses by name: 'Moses, Moses!' This is the inner or personal aspect of the revelation; it is not just a general truth that is being proclaimed, it is a word to Moses in the first instance, though a word that he will feel it his duty to pass on. Let us recall the lines I quoted from Hölderlin, about the poets who have to stand uncovered before the lightnings of God, to grasp the bolts in their hands and then pass them on, wrapped in human language![4] The divine voice then reveals the identity of the speaker: 'I am the God of your father, the God of Abraham and the God of Isaac and the God of Jacob.' These were the men of a former age, the patriarchs, we call them, the forebears of the Hebrews. Though Moses is the most significant human figure in the whole Hebrew-Israelite-Jewish experience, even he is not the founder, and broadly the same is true of all the mediators we are considering. There has already been a long time of preparation before the mediator can make his own weighty contribution. The next words are also of vital importance. God is not an abstract idea, but a God of men and women, the God of Abraham, Isaac and Jacob, likewise of Sarah, Rebecca and Rachel. So he has heard the cry of his people and will deliver them. He is not simply communicating knowledge to Moses, he is pointing him to a human situation which concerns God as well as the human beings involved in it. Moses' experience has some elements of mysticism in it, but it is also a typically prophetic experience, and we more naturally think of Moses as a prophet than as a mystic. The point is reinforced by the allusion to Moses and the people serving God 'on this mountain', when the monotheistic *doctrine* of the theophany would be welded to the ethical demands of the *law*.

As Moses continues to express his experience in words, new ways of understanding it find expression. He asks: 'Who am I that I should go to Pharaoh, and bring the sons of Israel out of Egypt?' This again is a moment common to many of the mediators – a moment of self-doubt, even of fear, a shrinking from the encounter with God and the obligations it lays upon them. The answer is that God himself will be with them. Obviously this answer can evoke faith but does not provide certainty.

Moses continues to raise doubts and questions. If the people of Israel ask him, 'What is the name of this God who has sent you?' what is he to reply? 'God said to Moses, "I AM WHO I AM . . . I AM has sent me to you.' This is the new name of God. What does it mean? It means that God is the fulness of being, not just another being, (like El Shaddai or El Elyon, names by which the Hebrews had called God before the time of Moses), but the ultimate Being beyond all beings which is also the source and power of their existence, the Being that lets them be, so that his first word was 'Let there be light', and in that first word-act of 'letting be' everything that is has the ground of its existence. As soon as one says that, then it is plain that there can be only one God, and that the many gods of ancient Egypt or any other polytheistic society are at best only personifications of the one true God. It is also plain that if this God is the fulness of being, then to say that HE IS is to say that he is goodness, he is truth, he is justice, yes, he is love and everything else that is affirmative, though when we use these words, we recognize their human limitations and when we refer them to God, we do so in an eminent sense that seeks to reach beyond the human sense.

Moses has the honour of being (in all probability) the first monotheist in history. Did Moses then intend and understand all these things we have just been saying? Probably not, for Moses was not primarily a philosopher. As I have said, we cannot adequately penetrate into what was in his mind in that experience of revelation. But we can ponder the words into which the revelation was put by Moses and the biblical writers who reported the incident, and I think we can honestly say that all that was said about God in the preceding paragraph was implicit in the I AM,[5] though it took many centuries and many thinkers (Philo, Maimonides, Aquinas, Hegel and a multitude of others) to unpack, and the task is perhaps not yet done. Of course, let me remind the reader that what Moses left us was not just an intellectual doctrine of God, but an *ethical* monotheism which calls for praxis as well as philosophy. But let no one use this as an excuse for devaluing or denigrating the intellectual task. Anti-intellectualism is one of the great weaknesses of religion at the present time.

But let us return to Moses' interpretative teaching that God's name is I AM or I AM WHO I AM or even I LET BE WHAT I LET BE. This new name is represented in the Hebrew Bible by four letters which in the Latin alphabet would be YHWH. This combination was probably pronounced Yahweh and is sometimes written thus in English translations of the Bible. In fact, however, the name of God was considered too sacred to pronounce, and a word meaning 'The Lord' was read instead. But the interesting point about the old word Yahweh is that it appears to be derived from the root of the Hebrew verb 'to be' (*hawah*) and so arose the theological reflections which relate God and Being. Yahweh is H E W H O I S, but he is in a sense that so transcends the 'isness' of finite beings that a whole line of theologians, from Dionysius the Areopagite to Paul Tillich have warned that even to speak of God as 'existing' can be misleading. In any case, Moses was persuaded by the shattering experience he had undergone. He still looked for excuses to avoid the task that had been laid on him, but eventually he went to the priest of Midian and asked leave to go back to his people in Egypt.

But when he got there, he experienced new difficulties. His own people were not enthusiastic. Perhaps they thought it was impossible to escape from Egypt, or perhaps they thought it was too dangerous, or possibly they were too lethargic and did not want to change a way of life to which they had become accustomed. It appears that there were channels of communication between the elders of the people, with whom Moses associated himself, and the Egyptian authorities. But when they made representations to Pharaoh, they were subjected to even more severe conditions of servitude. Naturally, they blamed Moses and his brother Aaron, who had become his spokesman. Pharaoh on his side hardened his attitude, no doubt suspecting that there were subversive stirrings among the slaves.

The continuation of the story is heavily steeped in legend. Exercising magical powers bestowed on him by Yahweh, Moses caused a series of plagues to strike the land of Egypt. Some of these plagues were simply natural disasters not uncommon in that part of the world. Such, for instance, were the plagues of gnats and flies and frogs. Others may have been picturesque exaggerations, such as the Nile turned to blood and the death of all the eldest sons in Egyptian families. All through this catalogue of disasters there is the constant message from Yahweh: 'Let my people go!'

It is understandable that in the mentality of those days, a series of disasters of the kind described might readily be interpreted as a sign of divine anger, and in this case, a sign of the anger of the God of the Hebrews. In spite of the plagues, the Egyptians would not let the people go, until the last one. Pharaoh at last relented when the eldest sons were slain, whatever actual event lies behind this plague. The final plague was also, according to the biblical account, the time when Moses instituted the great annual Israelite festival of the Passover, still observed by Jews to this day. There may have been a spring festival at this season already in earlier times, but it was now to be celebrated in memory of God's deliverance of his people from slavery. The fact that more than three thousand years after the event, it is still celebrated in the most important festival of the Jewish calendar, is strong evidence that some great event in the life of the people took place at that time, even if we find it impossible to accept the details given in the biblical account.

Returning to that account, we are told that the Israelites moved out from their homes in Egypt and headed eastward. Now came the most spectacular event of all in this history. The way was barred by the Red Sea, though the precise meaning of this expression is uncertain. It probably refers to some inlet at the northern end of the Red Sea, or perhaps just to some lake or marsh in that area. In the biblical account of the Israelites' crossing of the Red Sea, two versions have been combined together but are still distinguishable. One version describes an event that can be considered quite explicable in natural terms, though it came at just the right moment for the Israelites. The combination of a strong wind and a low tide caused the waters to recede, so that the Israelites were able to cross to the other side. The Egyptian army had meanwhile come in pursuit, but when soldiers tried to follow the Israelites across, their chariots stuck in the mud and the weight of their equipment prevented the crossing. The other version makes it all a supernatural miracle. By God's action through the agency of Moses, the waters are divided and stand like a wall on either side of the passage by which the Israelites are to cross. When the Egyptians follow, they are over-whelmed by the waters rushing back to cover up the pathway. The claim that this was a providential act of God does not depend on accepting the supernatural version of what happened, but the story does show very clearly how, in the context of a religious history, natural events are inflated into supernatural events. Nowadays we find these supernatural accounts incredible, but in the ancient world the introduction of the supernatural element was taken to be the evidence that God himself had been at work. At any rate, however we may understand these events, they were regarded as the high moment in the career of Moses and likewise the moment when the Hebrews were set free to become a people peculiarly devoted to God.

But the story of Moses has still a long way to go. We enter a third phase in his life which begins when he and the people enter the Sinai peninsula beyond the waters they had crossed. Tradition speaks of forty years of nomadic existence in various parts of the peninsula, and during these years Moses' leadership was a potent agency in welding the people into a definite community, with the worship of Yahweh as the principal bond that held them together. We are now to see the fulfilment of the words that had already been spoken at the burning bush: 'When you have brought the people out of Egypt, you shall serve God upon this mountain.' The mountain mentioned in that passage is Horeb and, although there is considerable uncertainty in the matter, Horeb has generally been identified with Sinai, a mountain in the south of the peninsula which bears the same name.

We pass over the various events that befell Moses and the people in the course of their journeyings through Sinai and come at once to the great moment at the mountain. Moses went up alone into the mountain and there he had again an encounter with God. The revelation which he received was that God willed to make a covenant with the people: 'Thus you shall say to the house of Jacob, and tell the people of Israel: you have seen what I did to the Egyptians, and how I bore you on eagles' wings and brought you to myself. Now, therefore, if you will obey my voice and keep my covenant you shall be my own possession among all peoples; for all the earth is mine, and you shall be to me a kingdom of priests and a holy nation.' Moses, the mediator, came down again from the mountain and conveyed God's message to the people. 'And all the people answered together and said, "All that the Lord has spoken we will do".' Moses reports this response back to Yahweh, and is then instructed to command the people to consecrate themselves and be ready on the third day for the Lord to come down on Mount Sinai.

Of course, we should recognize that this account was written quite a long time after the event, and has no doubt been idealized so that it tells us what the author thought should have happened, and this may not be the same as what actually happened. E. W. Nicholson acknowledges that there are differences of opinion about the antiquity of these verses. His own cautious view is that while the idea of a covenant between God and his people is not later than the eighth century, one cannot be confident that it was present in the earlier periods of Israelite history. He also makes the point that the event at Sinai (however we may describe it) was not, as has often been supposed, concerned with strengthening the relations of the human participants and making them a community, but was concerned primarily with the relation between Yahweh and the people.[6]

The biblical account goes on to tell that when the third day came, there were thunders and lightnings and a thick cloud over the mountain. 'And Mount Sinai was wrapped in smoke, because the Lord descended upon it in fire; and the smoke of it went up like the smoke of a kiln, and the whole mountain quaked greatly.' These phenomena are cited as supernatural manifestations of the presence of God. The people stood at the foot of the mountain, while Moses, accompanied by Aaron, went up to the summit to hear what the Lord would say. What he heard was the decalogue or Ten Commandments:

> I am the Lord your God, who brought you out of the land of Egypt,
> Out of the house of bondage.
> You shall have no other gods before me.
> You shall not make for yourself a graven image, or any likeness of anything that is in heaven above, or that is in the earth beneath, or that is in the water under the earth.
> You shall not take the name of the Lord your God in vain.
> Remember the sabbath day to keep it holy.
> Honour your father and your mother.
> You shall not kill.
> You shall not commit adultery.
> You shall not steal.
> You shall not bear false witness against your neighbour.
> You shall not covet your neighbour's house; you shall not covet your neighbour's wife, or his manservant, or his maidservant, or his ox, or his ass, or anything that is your neighbour's.

H. Jagersma writes that 'there is little reason to doubt that the decalogue (at least in a short form) could derive from the time of Moses'.[7] Many authorities would agree with this statement, though they would not be likely to agree in identifying the 'short form'. Admittedly, the Decalogue, basic though it is, is something of a mixture. Partly, it is a moral code, embodying some of the basic tenets of natural law. But partly it is also a religious code, and perhaps its religious injunctions were what mattered most to Moses and other early Israelites. It was monotheistic – no God but Yahweh. It was iconoclastic – the divine was not to be depicted visually. Then there was the institution of the sabbath – there was to be a sacred time, set apart for prayer and worship. Abraham Heschel has pointed out that in Judaism there are no cathedrals (sacred space) but the sabbath in some ways corresponds to a cathedral as sacred time.[8]

Since the time of the Enlightenment, we have tended to think of morality as independent of religion. That was certainly not Moses' view. For him, religion and morality were twined together. The moral commands were commands of God and expressed the Creator's will for his creatures. Though I think that nowadays we might want to express the relation of morality and religion in more sophisticated terms, I believe that the experiences of the past two hundred years or so has shown that it was a mistake to separate them so sharply.

Was Moses the first person in history to understand and teach ethical monotheism? I suppose we could say that he was the first person to put it on the map, so to speak, and to secure for it a base in Israel from which there has come a continuous tradition ever since. We do not quite know what Moses believed or just how pure his monotheism was, and it may be conceded that very likely the biblical accounts of him have been idealized in the light of Israel's later beliefs. But that could happen only because these later prophets of Israel recognized in Moses a kindred spirit, indeed, the pioneer from whom their own beliefs and insights were originally derived. One may recognize that very probably Moses did not have such a clear conception of monotheism or the vision of a universal religion as did the post-exilic prophets of a thousand years later. But Moses was the one who had made the decisive turn in that direction. Just as I remarked earlier that Moses' conception of God as I AM has implicit in it ideas which he himself did not think out but which were waiting to be unpacked by thinkers of later times, so on the religious side the level of ethical monotheism which he had attained was already determinative for the future developments of Israelite and Jewish religion, and eventually for Christianity and Islam as well.

Where did Moses learn his monotheism? It has sometimes been suggested that its origins lay in the religious innovations of the heretic Pharaoh Akhenaten who flourished about the middle of the fourteenth century BCE, that is to say, roughly a century before the exodus. We recall that Moses had an Egyptian name, was brought up at the Egyptian court, was apparently taken to be an Egyptian by the people of Midian when he fled there. So there might be a case that he had learned about the religious reforms of Akhenaten, who abol-

ished the old gods of Egypt and put in their place the worship of the
one god, namely, the solar disc (Aten).[9] But the theory has very little
evidence to support it. Moses' monotheism is quite different from
Akhenaten's. Yahweh, the God of Moses, is not associated with the
sun and indeed the second commandment forbids any visible
representation of God. Furthermore, it seems that Akhenaten's
reforms made hardly any impact, even in court circles, and would
hardly be remembered in Moses' time.

It is much more plausible to believe that Moses' monotheism arose
out of his own religious experience and his reflections on it.
Similarities in different religions or similarities among the mediators
of faith seem to rise spontaneously and independently, and are not
necessarily derived one from another. If we think of Moses, despite
his early date, as perhaps the first significant figure of the axial age
then we shall be content to think that his experiences and beliefs, like
those of later mediators, arose out of a deepening of human
experience on a worldwide scale, in response, we may believe, to the
impact of a universal Spirit.

Moses is reputed to have had a very long life, and he had many
further adventures after the great moment of Sinai. We have already
noticed that the people were not always too ready to obey him or to
accept his teaching, and we get the impression that in those years of
nomadic existence in the wilderness, there was much discontent and
the smoulderings of rebellion. Everyone is familiar with the story of
how, even while Moses was communing with God on the mountain-
top, the people, apparently with the connivance of Aaron, made
themselves an idol in the shape of a golden calf. Obviously it was
going to take a very long time to wean them away from the visible
gods to which they had been accustomed, and to replace these idols
with the imageless I AM of prophetic religion.

Moses quelled the rebellion that had produced the golden calf, but
there was still unrest. While Moses had his conversations with God
and dreamed of leading the people into the promised land of Canaan
where their ancestor, Abraham and the other patriarchs, had
sojourned many centuries before, the people grew increasingly
impatient with their harsh nomadic life. Moses never entered
Canaan, though he saw it from the mountains east of the Jordan. The
circumstances of his death are obscure. He died and was buried in the
land of Moab, 'but no man knows the place of his burial to this day'.
A German biblical scholar speculated that Moses was finally killed

by his own people in the course of a rebellion. This speculation was taken up by Freud, who saw Moses as the type of the father-figure, both admired and hated by the children who eventually kill him, and then blot out the memory of what has happened.[10] Freud's view is fantastic, but if we are going to indulge in fantasy, I prefer to go to a Jewish apocryphal document, written about the time of Jesus and called *The Assumption of Moses.*[11] It exists only in fragmentary form, but appears to have given an account of Moses' end more worthy of a mediator. He was assumed into heaven, and it is promised that at the end of the age all the people of Israel will follow him thither.

2

Zoroaster

(628–551 BCE)

In a mountainous region of western Iran stands a precipitous rock, known as the rock of Bisitun (anciently Behistun) after the name of a nearby village. In about 1835 an English officer in the service of the East India Company discovered an ancient inscription on the sheer face of this rock. The inscription had been caused to be placed there by the Persian emperor, Darius I, probably not long after the beginning of his reign in 522 BCE. The inscription was trilingual, the languages being Akkadian, Elamite and Old Persian, and the script being various types of cuneiform. Considerable linguistic information was gained from the discovery, but what is of chief interest from the point of view of this book is that it gives us attestation that the religion of Zoroaster was apparently well established by the time, at least in imperial circles.

The relevant part of the inscription runs as follows:

[Says Darius the king:] For this reason Ahura Mazda bore me aid, and the other gods who are, because I was not disloyal, I was not a follower of the lie (*drug*), I did not do wrong – neither I nor my family. I walked in justice. Neither to the weak nor to the mighty did I do wrong . . . You who shall be king hereafter – the man who follows the lie or who shall do wrong, be not a friend to them but punish them well.[1]

Ahura Mazda was the name which Zoroaster used for God, and although it is believed that this name was used in the older Iranian religion, Ninian Smart points out that it had not appeared in earlier inscriptions, including those of Cyrus, who was Darius' immediate predecessor on the throne.[2] It looks as if Ahura Mazda had acquired a new prestige, and this indeed happened in the teaching of Zoroaster, who did not invent Ahura Mazda but did claim that he is the one true God and at the same time a God of righteousness. Other features of the Bisitun inscription also point to the influence of Zoroaster, for instance, the language about 'followers of the lie' and the strongly ethical emphasis. Zoroaster may share with Moses the distinction of being one of the earliest mediators who taught an ethical monotheism. It may be, of course, that when we look more closely at his teaching, we may question whether it was a pure monotheism. But I think it could be fairly said that Zoroaster achieved for the worship of Ahura Mazda something very like what Moses achieved for the worship of Yahweh.

Darius the Great was not the son of Cyrus, though he is said to have been related. His own father was a provincial governor in the eastern part of the country. The father's name was (in the form used by Greek historians) Hystaspes, and he is important because, according to the tradition, he was probably Zoroaster's most notable convert. Darius seems to have been brought up in the religion that his father had learned from Zoroaster and ensured that it was to be the state religion of Persia. However, although he seems to have had a strong attachment to the newly emerging faith, he followed the tolerant policies of Cyrus in allowing the subject peoples of his empire to continue in their traditional beliefs.

When a person of deep religious insight appears, attention is at first centred on the teaching, and only later does a biographical interest arise. This is the case with Zoroaster, as with most of our other mediators. There are, in consequence, wide differences of opinion about the date of his life and activity. In Hellenistic times, the *magi* or wise men of Persia were regarded with a kind of superstitious awe. Aristotle thought that they antedated even Egyptian civilization, and since Zoroaster himself was popularly regarded as the principal *magus*, he was assigned an impossibly early date, 5000 BCE or earlier.[3] Some modern scholars believe that he was active some time between 1400 and 800. This early dating would allow him to be a contemporary of Moses or of other early Hebrew prophets, though it does not seem likely that Zoroaster influenced the prophets of Israel or that they influenced him.

To assign a very early date to Zoroaster makes it difficult to explain the apparently sudden rise of the new (or newly reformed) faith in the sixth century BCE and there are also various Zoroastrian traditions which favour a later date. These traditions are complicated, but the chronology they suggest is credible. The conversion of Hystaspes is taken as a base, and is reputed to have taken place two hundred and fifty-eight years before the conquest of Persia by Alexander the Great. Zoroaster was forty years old at the time, so we arrive at 628 BCE as his year of birth. The honour of being his birthplace is claimed by Rayy (anciently Rhages), now a suburb of Teheran but in Zoroaster's time a rural area.

Of the various stories told about Zoroaster, some are obviously legends of a kind that usually attach themselves to great religious figures. Such are the accounts of a miraculous birth initiated by fire sent from heaven; of failed attempts by shadowy enemies to kill the child; of miracles performed by him in his youth, and so on. Less likely to be fabrications are the traditions that he grew up in a cattle-rearing community and that he became a priest. His interest in religion and his turn to monotheism may have been produced by influences similar to those in Moses' background – the vast empty spaces of the Middle East and the wide skies. Even today, Iran, though it has more than ten times the area of England, has less than half the population, and more than two thousand years ago it must have been very sparsely populated outside the few cities.

A further parallel with Moses is provided by the revelatory experience granted to Zoroaster when he was thirty. At dawn he had gone down to the bank of a river to offer a libation. He was confronted by a supernatural figure who addressed to him several questions. 'Who are you? What is your chief desire? In what are you diligent?' He replied, 'I am Zoroaster. My chief desire is righteousness. My wish is to become aware of the two existences'. He was conducted into the heavenly assembly and placed in the seat of those who seek instruction. From Ahura Mazda ('Spirit of Wisdom') he was shown the duality of the original principles, and told that Angra Mainyu ('Hostile Spirit') had in the beginning chosen the evil course, whilst Ahura Mazda had chosen righteousness.[4]

This account of the revelation comes from a relatively late Zoroastrian text, though it must embody early traditions. But no doubt it has been made more dramatic (a statement that Zoroaster continued to be instructed for ten more years may indicate that the conversion experience was quite a gradual one) and some points are probably exaggerated in the telling of it. An example of this would be the stress on the duality of principles, for although an awareness of the evil principle and its personification in Angra Mainyu seems to go back to Zoroaster himself, the elevation of this into a metaphysical dualism comes only later.

After the ten years of further pondering on religion, Zoroaster was told by Ahura Mazda to go to the court of Hystaspes in order to proclaim there the true religion. Hystaspes was ready to receive him and eager to learn more about God and the life of the spirit, but his mind was prejudiced against Zoroaster by the *karbs*, priests of the old religion who feared that their position was being undermined. However, Zoroaster was able (not without a few alleged miracles) to overcome the opposition, and Hystaspes embraced the faith and by teaching it to his son Darius was the means of making the religion of Zoroaster one of the great faiths of the world.[5]

Opposition, however, continued. Indeed, as we shall see, Zoroastrianism may with some plausibility claim to have been the most persecuted faith in all history. Zoroaster himself is said to have been celebrating the fire ceremony in honour of Ahura Mazda when he was stabbed to death by a *karb*. When this happened, he was seventy-seven years old, and the year would be approximately 551 BCE.

The foregoing sketch of the career of Zoroaster, it must be apparent to the reader, contains very few 'facts', for the material just does not exist. Although I have leaned as far as possible toward the traditional accounts, I am well aware that perhaps an equally good case could be made for saying that he lived two or three hundred years earlier and that we know nothing certain about him! I have left out of account other arguments based on the language of the oldest Zoroastrian texts, since these arguments can be properly assessed only by a small group of experts.

But even if one were able to appreciate the linguistic evidence concerning the earliest Zoroastrian material, what arguments could be based on it for settling questions about Zoroaster's date or the scene of his activities? It has been pointed out by several writers that the language of the early texts is that of north-west Iran, while the tradition associates Zoroaster with the eastern part of the country. But can one draw any firm conclusions from this? Prophets, after all, are mobile. Perhaps they have to be mobile, for we may recall the statement in John's Gospel 'that a prophet has no honour in his own country'. As far as Zoroaster is concerned, we are told that he did indeed leave his own country, wherever it was, to obey the command of Ahura Mazda that he should go to the country of Hystaspes. I wonder also whether language barriers would have been a sufficient difficulty in preventing someone with a message which he believed to be a divine commission from going to a strange territory. Just as today in Europe the citizen of any given country will probably have quite a good knowledge of the languages of two or three neighbouring countries, so in ancient western Asia many people would be proficient in several languages. The trilingual inscription mentioned earlier in this chapter would seem to suggest as much.[6]

The arguments about the historical Zoroaster will no doubt go on, for there is at present not enough evidence to reach a definite conclusion, and it is unlikely that there ever will be such evidence. However, there can be no reasonable doubt that there was indeed a real human being who radically reformed the religion of ancient Persia and whose labours resulted in the rise and continuance for many centuries of the religion we call Zoroastrianism. So we may leave these disputed questions of history and turn to the teaching of the prophet.

But now we find ourselves confronted with new difficulties. The problem now is not a shortage of material but rather a superfluity. There is a vast number of Zoroastrian scriptures produced over many centuries, and the problem is to know what can be ascribed to Zoroaster himself and what was the work of later disciples. Sometimes, of course, the later work may reflect or be a genuine development from Zoroaster's own thoughts. But sometimes – as happens in every religion – the new material is a departure from the intentions of the originator of the tradition or even a corruption. If, as is generally believed, Zoroaster intended to move Persian religion in the direction of an ethical monotheism, then there were undoubtedly periods when his successors moved away from this. We have noted already the superstitious regard in which the *magi* were held in Hellenistic times, when Zoroastrianism was associated with magic and the occult. At other times, there were recrudescences of the old polytheism.

Texts from the different periods have become interwoven with one another in the form of liturgies. One benefit of this is that liturgies are memorized, especially by priests and are recited without change over long periods of time. Thus even when texts are not written down, they may be preserved orally. In Zoroastrianism, the collection of sacred texts is called the *Zend Avesta*. Embedded in the liturgies are a number of ancient hymns, known as the *Gathas*, which probably go back to Zoroaster himself and constitute the primary source for his teaching. But there is also much later teaching, some of which may derive ultimately from Zoroaster, and some of which may throw light on earlier teachings. The various traditions mentioned in the earlier historical part of this chapter were drawn from later parts of the Zoroastrian *corpus*, and therefore, as I have acknowledged, must be regarded with caution.

The recovery of Zoroaster's teaching is further complicated by the many persecutions to which the religion was subjected. I mentioned earlier that it must be about the most persecuted religion in history, and I had not forgotten the Jews when I wrote that. The first great setback came after the conquest of Persia by Alexander the Great, following his victory at Issus in 333 BCE. There was a great slaughter of Zoroastrian priests, and since at that time the ancient texts had not been written down and were preserved orally by the priesthood, this amounted to a grievous loss of ancient material. The really devastating moment came about 636 CE, when the armies of Islam swept into the country. Although the official policy of Islam was to tolerate traditional religions, there was from this time onward a steady pressure on the Zoroastrian religion, sometimes erupting into actual persecution. The writing was on the wall for Zoroastrianism – a somewhat ironic fate, for Zoroaster's achievement in Iran was in many ways similar to what Muhammad achieved in Arabia. However, Zoroastrianism survived in spite of all, though as a very reduced remnant. One important factor in the survival was the determined effort of the believers to recover and preserve as far as was possible the texts that had been lost or destroyed.

We can therefore still reconstruct the outlines of Zoroaster's faith. In seeking to do this, we may let ourselves be guided by what is in effect a Zoroastrian creed, assent to which, according to Professor Mary Boyce, was probably required of converts in the early days. I quote the opening verse:

> I profess myself a Mazda-worshipper, a follower of Zoroaster, opposing the *daevas*, accepting the Ahuric doctrine; one who praises the Amesha Spentas, who worships the Amesha Spentas. To Ahura Mazda, the good, rich in treasures, I ascribe all things good, to the Just One, splendid, glorious.

The creed or confession goes on to renounce evils of various kinds and to profess loyalty to Ahura Mazda and goodwill to his worshippers.[7]

The first item in the creed then is belief in Ahura Mazda. When we turn to the *Gathas*, two things seem to be clearly taught about Ahura Mazda – he is the creator of all that is and he is the Just One. In a long *Gatha* of twenty stanzas, these points are made repeatedly. To quote just four lines, where both ideas come together:

> This I ask of thee, O Ahura Mazda; answer me well;
> Who at the creation was the first father of justice?
> Who assigned their path to the sun and the stars?
> Who decreed the waxing and waning of the moon, if it was not Thee?[8]

What perhaps is not so clearly stated is that Ahura Mazda is the one and only God. Does this need to be explicit stated, or is it already implied in the thought of the transcendent Creator? Or is it the case that Zoroaster was still willing to find a place for minor deities alongside the Wise Lord?[9] He does in fact recognize a group of seven spiritual beings, sometimes called by students of Zoroastrianism the 'Heptad'. Sometimes Ahura Mazda himself seems to be one of the seven, but he has an *alter ego*, Spenta Mainyu (Holy Spirit) and it is in this form that he is reckoned a member of the Heptad. Perhaps what we are seeing in these ideas is the emergence of a pure monotheism out of a polytheistic matrix. It is quite possible to think of these seven spirits often called the Amesha Spentas, as personified attributes of the one God. When their names are translated into English, they are the names of virtues or spiritual qualities – Right, Health, Devotion and such like. It was one of them who met Zoroaster at the river and took him to the heavenly assembly to receive his revelation, and the name of that holy intermediary is translated as 'Good Thought'. So it seems reasonable to accept that the seven members of the Heptad are not minor deities but personified activities of one God. There is something comparable in the early parts of the Hebrew scriptures, where God and the Angel of the Lord seem on occasion to be the same person; or to the Jewish belief that there are seven archangels, or the Christian mention in the Apocalypse of the seven spirits of God. Whether these several ideas are connected with the Persian doctrine of the Heptad need not concern us.

There is, however, another class of spiritual beings recognized by Zoroaster, namely, the *daevas*. These may have been minor deities in the old Iranian religion, and it seems that sacrifices had been offered to them, but Zoroaster demanded that such sacrifices cease. The *daevas* are to be opposed, not worshipped. These *daevas* seem to be rather like the jinns in Islam, spirits that could hardly be considered even minor gods, but not necessarily evil demons. But in several religions of the near and middle east, including early Christianity, the old gods of heathendom were not simply abolished but reconceived as evil spirits.

This remark brings us to another figure who appears in the *Gathas*, Angra Mainyu, the 'Hostile Spirit'. Was he perhaps originally a god, who became a fallen angel, or was he formerly one of the Amesha Spentas in some earlier way of naming the members of the Heptad? The question is not so idle as it sounds, because it again makes us ask about the purity of Zoroaster's monotheism. Was it really a dualism, in which Angra Mainyu leads the forces of evil as an independent power comparable to Ahura Mazda himself? Or is Angra Mainyu a creature of Ahura Mazda, on a lower level of being than the supreme God? The language of the *Gathas* is somewhat ambiguous on this point:

Truly, there are two primal spirits, twins renowned to be in conflict. In thought and word, in act, they are two; the better and the bad.

Reading this, and noting the expressions, 'two primal spirits' and 'twins', we might well think that Ahura Mazda and Angra Mainyu are equiprimordial and that there are two conflicting sources of the creation. Yet this would conflict with the teaching that the created order is the work of Ahura Mazda. Most interpreters believe that Zoroaster himself regarded Ahura Mazda as the ultimate God, but that later Zoroastrianism tended in the direction of a metaphysical dualism in which the good and evil principles are alike eternal and equally poised. To be sure, it seems to have been in the very dawn of the world that the conflict began. But if one denies the ultimacy to Ahura Mazda, one would surely need to posit a third spirit who had created both Ahura Mazda and Angra Mainyu.

What is the place of human beings in this scheme? They are called to range themselves on one side or the other in the cosmic struggle. Just as in the beginning, Ahura Mazda chose righteousness (*asha*) while Angra Mainyu chose the lie (*drug*), so every human being is faced with a basic choice. If he or she chooses to pursue the right, then he co-operates with Ahura Mazda; but whoever chooses the way of the lie will be a follower of Angra Mainyu and will eventually come to the 'worst existence', that is to say, hell.

Assuming that Zoroaster's own dualism was relative rather than absolute, how do we appraise it? On the credit side, we can admit that he takes evil very seriously. In that respect, he would seem to be close to the other near- or middle-eastern religions, Judaism, Christianity and Islam. If one is habitually thinking of the world as a cosmic battleground where good and evil are constantly opposing each other, then perhaps this does encourage moral sensitivity and makes one aware of the responsibility that accompanies our free decisions. But on the negative side, there is a tendency to divide the human race into two hostile and competing sections, the righteous and the wicked, the followers of the Lord and the followers of the devil. We meet something like this in the Hebrew Psalms, where the godly and the ungodly are set over against one another and even, on occasion, the ungodly are anathematized. This hardly makes for peace among human beings. But again we can discern influences in Zoroaster's experience which led him to such beliefs. The peaceful cow-herding community in which he had grown up had often been harassed and persecuted by lawless nomadic tribes. Perhaps this is how he was first impressed by the difference between *ash*, 'truth' or 'order', and *drug*, 'the lie'. But there was grave danger in transferring so directly the choice of Ahura Mazda and Angra Mainyu to human beings, for it introduces what might be called the 'them and us' mentality that has been so injurious in the history of religions, though it ought to be said in mitigation that the Zoroastrians have more often than not been on the receiving end of persecution.

Although Zoroaster, as we have seen, adopts a harsh attitude toward those who become children of the lie by following Angra Mainyu rather than Ahura Mazda, there is a gentler side to his teaching, in some passages, almost a praise of weakness. These passages return to the symbolism of the peaceful cow-herding community. Its order and tranquillity contrast with the violence of the raiding nomadic tribes. Not just the cowherds but the oxen themselves are made to represent the faithful followers of right-eousness, persecuted by those who have chosen the lie. Zoroaster gives a voice to the cattle in the person of the Ox-soul, whose lowing he interprets as a naive prayer addressed to the creator:

For whom didst thou shape me? Who fashioned me? Fury and

raiding hold me captive, cruelty and might. For me there is no pastor but thou. Then appear to me with a good pasturage![10]

A prayer of Zoroaster from another *Gatha* is closely related to the prayer of the cattle:

> Who is found as protector of my cattle, who for myself, but truth and thee, Lord Mazda, and Good Thought, my invocation having been heard. Truly praising, I shall worship you all, O Mazda, with Truth and Good Thought and Power. Truly I shall vow myself and be, O Mazda, your praiser as long as I have force and strength.[11]

There is a strong eschatological note in Zoroaster's teaching, and some scholars have believed that its influence was important for both Judaism and Christianity. If some of his teaching raises doubts about the sovereignty of Ahura Mazda over Angra Mainyu, these doubts are dispelled by the vision of the end when the victory of the good powers over the evil ones will be complete. Zoroaster had taught that some of his followers would be not only good but better than good, and such a follower was called a *saoshyant* which may be translated 'saviour'. We could think of a person deserving this title as one who not only follows the teaching of Zoroaster but draws others to follow it and to gain their salvation. The prophet seemed to expect that a great *saoshyant* would arise in the future and co-operate with Ahura Mazda in bringing in the new age. The passages summarized below give a clear idea of this eschatology. They are not from the *Gathas* but from later texts which are, however, believed to stay close to Zoroaster's own views. A belief in resurrection was already present in the old Iranian religion which had held sway before Zoroaster's time, and which he adapted to accord with his own teaching.

Zoroaster asks Ahura Mazda how the body can be reassembled once it has been dissolved. Ahura Mazda replies that Zoroaster already believes that the wonders of creation have come about through the divine agency. Why then should he doubt that the Lord of Wisdom can also make again that which once was and has since disappeared? In the due time, the *Saoshyant* will raise the dead, both the righteous and the wicked. They will be brought together in a great assembly where each one will behold his own deeds, both good deeds and bad deeds, and 'the just will stand out among the wicked like white sheep among black'. Next, fire will sweep through the earth like a river of molten metal, purifying the just and destroying the wicked. Finally, the Evil Spirit, Angra Mainyu, 'helpless and with his power destroyed, will rush back to shadowy darkness through the way by which he entered [the world]'. That way will then be sealed up. It is a fairly grim picture, though not more so than the Revelation of John. I suppose that both Zoroaster's picture and John's brought some hope to helpless victims of persecution.

The eschatology just described gives an important place to fire, and this may be something inherited from the old religion. Zoroaster seems to have prized the symbol as representing both the purging of the believer and the punishment of the wicked, and both he and his followers have found a place for a fire ceremony in their reformed religion.

We have already noted that the spiritual heirs of Zoroaster suffered persecution in the Hellenistic period and again under Islam. The story of oppression continued. Under continuing Muslim harassment, some Zoroastrians in the ninth and tenth centuries CE emigrated to India and settled in the region of Gujarat. The Muslims arrived there too in the fifteenth century, but when the British came to India, there was respite and the Zoroastrians (known in India as Parsees) found a haven in Bombay. That city is still the major concentration of Zoroastrians, though there are only about 100,000 of them. In Iran itself, there are about 5000. A few have emigrated to North America. One cannot help asking why a religion whose prophet had a vision that might have had universal appeal has numerically declined so greatly. No doubt there are several reasons. The religion itself has frequently fallen away from Zoroaster's ideals, it has, as we have seen, been subjected to major persecutions, and it remained so closely bound to the Persian nation that when it encountered in Islam a truly global religion, it could not maintain itself. But although it could not be called a world religion Zoroastrianism and especially Zoroaster himself have an honoured place among the faiths that have most enriched the spiritual life of mankind.

These remarks prompt a further comparison with the religion of Israel. There too lay the possibility of a universal faith, but in fact Judaism is in the main the religion of a particular ethnic group, and Judaism has also suffered centuries of persecution even to the point of attempted genocide. In spite of all, Judaism has about 18 million adherents; so as far as numbers are concerned, it is much stronger than Zoroastrianism. But why have these two relatively small groups attracted so much hostility? The answer, it seems to me, lies in the fact that they both teach an ethical monotheism. For the powerful of the earth, that is a subversive doctrine. For the tyrants of all ages, from the ancient emperors down to the commonplace modern dictators, the Hitlers and Stalins of the twentieth century, the teaching that their power and the power of the state are not absolute and that there is a just God in heaven is bad news, and those who disseminate it must be liquidated.

This chapter may fittingly end by quoting the tribute which in his Gifford Lectures Bishop Gore paid to Zoroaster and the faith named after him:

> Clearly it is not possible to suggest that this lofty religion – however closely resembling the Jewish faith – could have been borrowed from the Jews, nor is there any other alien source to which it can be attributed. It remains in its lofty severity a momentous creation, if it be not wiser to call it, as Zoroaster himself would have called it, a signal inspiration by the divine Spirit of an individual prophet. It exhibits, at a very early stage in the history of mankind, a clear conception of the good life for man. It is puritanical – that is, it has no flavouring of art and gives but few signs of accommodation to ordinary human desires for relaxation and enjoyment; but it is in the highest degree lofty and inspiring, and full as it is of the sense of pity for the oppressed and miserable, it can rightly call itself a gospel; further, it is conspicuous for the simplicity and decision with which (on the basis of a highly ambiguous tradition) it exhibits in the boldest outline the theology by which this good life is controlled and justified, and the eschatology by which it is supported. The longer one thinks about Zoroaster's religion and allows it to absorb one's mind, the more central, the more illuminating, the more divine it appears. But in fact, if it was truly a light shining in a dark place, it shone in its purity but for a very little while and in a very restricted area.[12]

Unfortunately it is rare to find someone who spent his life in one communion paying such handsome tribute to the inspirer of another communion so different from his own. But this openness to one another without deserting one's own source of light is precisely what is demanded of the religions today and is the goal toward which this study of the mediators is directed.

3

Lao-zu

(604–510 BCE)

As accords with its status as the most populous nation on earth, China claims two of our mediators, as well as having made major contributions to the development of the religion of Buddha in its Mahayana form. The two indigenous Chinese mediators are Lao-zu and Confucius. Lao-zu is perhaps the most obscure of all the nine key-figures of religion to be studied in this book. In part, this was due to deliberate self-effacement arising out of his philosophy, for in his way of thinking, it is the cosmos or the total of all that exists that really deserves our study, rather than things or persons arising out of that whole. So we have only the most meagre details of Lao-zu's life, and although there has survived his world-famous book, the *Tao Te Ching*, it tells us virtually nothing about the life and times of its author.

It will not therefore surprise us that some sceptical historians have held that Lao-zu never existed. They point out that his name is probably not a personal name at all, but a title, namely, 'Old Master'. But such scepticism overreaches itself. As I mentioned, we have this remarkable book, the *Tao Te Ching*. Even the most sceptical historian will hardly claim that it dropped directly from heaven. This means there must have been one or more human thinkers who composed it some time around the middle of the first millennium BCE. To express the same thing in different words, there must have been an Old Master, that is to say, a Lao-zu, living around that time, even if we do not know what his name was. In the case of very influential people, the title sometimes displaces the personal name. We talk, for instance, of 'Buddha' and 'Christ', as if these were the names of men, whereas in fact they are titles, meaning respectively 'the enlightened one' and 'the anointed one'. It so happens that in these two cases we know the personal names, Siddhartha Gautama and Jesus of Nazareth.

Perhaps we also know the name of the Old Master, Lao-zu. The Chinese historian Si-ma Qien[1] wrote an account of the sage's life about 100 BCE, based presumably on traditional material. Lao-zu's name before he earned his honorific title, was Li Er, his birthplace was a town now known as Luyi, in Honan province, central China, and the year of his birth was 604 BCE. He spent his life as an archivist in the service of the ruler of one of the many small states into which China was divided at that time. One interesting event in the career of Lao-zu was his meeting with his much younger contemporary, Confucius. This is said to have occurred in the year 517, when Confucius was thirty-four and Lao-zu had reached a venerable eighty-seven. They are said to have talked about ceremonies, a major theme in Chinese religions.

In spite of the differences between the two men, Lao-zu seems to have made quite an impression on Confucius. The latter is quoted as having said to his disciples after the interview: 'I know how birds can fly, fishes swim, and animals run. The runner may be snared, the swimmer hooked, and the flyer shot by an arrow. But there is the dragon. I cannot tell how he mounts on the wind through the clouds and rises to heaven. Today I have seen Lao-zu, and can compare him only to the dragon.'[2]

The end of Lao-zu is, like the life that had gone before it, shrouded in mystery. He is reputed to have reached a great age (it may be that the reports of his longevity are the source for the belief among followers of popular Taoism that it lengthens one's life). But as we have seen that he was already in his late eighties at the time of Confucius' visit, it is unlikely that he could have lived for more than about a decade after. So his death must have occurred *c.* 510. But it is here that the mystery arises. According to Si-ma, Lao-zu lived on at the state capital becoming increasingly discouraged as he saw the society around him changing for the worse, as he believed. He finally decided to leave his native place and withdraw to the west.

He had to pass through a gate leading westward, and there he was stopped by the warden of the gate, and told that before he could continue on his journey, he would have to compose a book, setting out his thoughts. This was the legendary origin of the *Tao Te Ching*. Lao-zu wrote his book of about 5000 characters. This means it is a very short book, much shorter than the shortest of the Christian Gospels, St Mark's. When he had completed his task,

Lao-zu was permitted to continue on his westward way and, so it is said, was never seen again.

But plainly contradicting the story just told is another one, told by one of Lao-zu's greatest disciples, Juang-zu. When Lao-zu died, Kuan Shih went to condole with his son, but after crying out three times, he came out. The disciples said to him, 'Were you not a friend of the Master?' Kuan Shih replied that he had indeed been a friend, but he had been quite upset by what he had seen. Old men were wailing and young men were wailing, but this expression of grief was so contrary to the spirit of the Master's own teaching that he must have taught it badly. 'When the Master came, it was at the proper time: when he went away, it was the simple sequence of his coming. Quiet acquiescence in what happens at its proper time, and quietly submitting [to its ceasing] afford no occasion for grief or for joy.'[3]

The two stories of the end of Lao-zu are, as I have said, contradictory, at least, if one takes them in a simple literal sense. The first story may strike us as having a more legendary character than the second, especially in its proffered explanation of the writing of the *Tao Te Ching*. The second story is more natural, and might even have originated in a reminiscence of the occasion, passed on by a relative of the deceased, for Si-ma Qien claims that direct descendents of the Old Master were still living in his time, and that was long after Juang-zu. On the other hand, one might think that the story of the mourning was told simply as a way of illustrating the Taoist teaching that one should take the good with the bad *aequo animo*. One further small point of information may help to strengthen the claims of the second 'more natural' version of the end of Lao-zu. I am told that in his native city of Luyi there is still a temple allegedly built over the resting place of his remains. Such local traditions do not arise out of nothing.

I think, however, that Martin Palmer may have provided a satisfactory explanation that solves the problem of the two contradictory reports of Lao-zu's end. According to Palmer, to 'go to the west' was simply a euphemism for dying: 'In Chinese mythology, the West was the land of wonders and of the afterlife.'[4] So the story about Lao-zu leaving the city is just a poetic way of saying that he died in Luyi, and was probably buried there.

So what of the further claim that he wrote his 5000 word treatise in order to get through the gate? It may be a roundabout way of confirming what has often been suggested by scholars, namely, that the *Tao Te Ching* was not in fact written by Lao-zu in his lifetime, but was put together after his death by disciples who recalled sayings of the Master and wished to preserve them. The process may have gone on for a hundred years or more, and inevitably some of the material would be altered and some sayings from sages other than the Master would come to be included. This would account for inconsistencies and any other traces of multiple authorship in the work, but it would not call for abandonment of the tradition that the book conveys the essential teaching of 'Lao-zu', however we may decide to understand that designation. It does seem that the book was in existence and was known to Juang-zu, whose *floruit* is placed about the middle of the fourth century BCE, that is to say, about 200 years after the activity of the Master. Western readers will notice that there is a parallel between such an account of the origin of the *Tao Te Ching* and the Christian Gospels. According to those New Testament scholars who embrace form criticism, after the death of Jesus and the lapse of perhaps thirty or forty years, some of the disciples began to set down in writing sayings and incidents from his life, as preserved in the tradition, and the composition of these Gospels, from Mark to John, went on for another generation.

When I quoted earlier the passage from Si-ma Qien in which he sketched the career of Lao-zu, I confined myself to the remarks in which he purports to give information about events of the sage's life, and deliberately omitted for later consideration what was in fact Si-ma's most important sentence: 'Lao-zu cultivated the Tao and its attributes.' So although I have tried to show in the foregoing paragraphs that the historical traditions about Lao-zu are not to be lightly dismissed as mere fabrications, I fully acknowledge that they are very doubtful, and that the really important point about Lao-zu, however we may understand that designation, is that he or someone else 'cultivated the Tao' and that the thoughts then entertained on the subject were eventually included in the book we know as the *Tao Te Ching*. If critical historians think I have been too credulous about the tradition, let me confess that I am respectful of tradition, but my main motive for trying to elucidate the historical background of each of these mediators is, as I explained in the introduction, a theological one. It is important to see these mediators as human beings like ourselves, and we have to struggle against the common tendency to elevate them so far that they escape from the human sphere altogether. But when that happens – and something like that did happen to Lao-zu as also to most of the others – the true character of a mediator is destroyed, for the genuine mediator between God and man must not only have an intimate relation to God but must be firmly rooted in the human race.

So what can we say about the *Tao Te Ching*? Very little, it would seem, for most of my readers will know at least that stern warning in the opening sentence of the book: 'The Tao that can be spoken is not the real Tao.'[5] This is the kind of language that we meet in mystics of all cultural backgrounds, Eastern or Western. The Tao is like the One of Plotinus – it is the ultimate reality on which all else depends for existence, but it is not itself another existent thing, but prior to everything. It is therefore nameless, and to us who are accustomed to think only of the entities we meet within the realm of space and time, the One or the Tao is so elusive, so far beyond our power to imagine or conceive, that we are tempted to think it is nothing at all. Yet in spite of all this, the mystic has to speak of it, for although he cannot find a name or frame a description, this reality has somehow touched him and deeply impressed itself on him. It has become the most important factor in his life and we soon find Lao-zu giving it a name: The Greatest!

The basic meaning of the word '*tao*' in Chinese is 'way'. So the way or road between two cities is a '*tao*'. Like the English word 'way', the Chinese '*tao*' is used metaphorically for the way of life. Confucius often uses the term, but usually in this practical sense for a way of life and for the ethical questions which arise in life. Lao-zu, however, uses the word in a metaphysical or ontological sense. I believe that the word '*tao*' has been used in some versions of the Bible in Chinese to translate *logos*. I suppose in some ways the Tao and the *logos* could both be considered as governing principles in the universe, but it might seem that the word *logos* has connotations of 'logic' that do not belong to the more mystical and incomprehensible nature of the Tao. One might also compare the Tao with the notion of being in the philosophy of Heidegger.[6] In that philosophy, Being is not any existing thing or entity, so that in a sense it is nothing. Yet Being is that which lets everything be, not by way of creation (in this there is also agreement with Lao-zu) but simply by letting the beings be. I doubt if even emanation would be a good word to express the relation of being to beings, or the Tao to the existing things of the universe. But I shall come back to this point. Among Christian mystics, the idea of a 'God beyond God' could possibly be compared to the Tao. It is found in Dionysius the Areopagite, and reappears in modern theology in the writings of Tillich, though he could hardly be called a mystic. But if one wishes to have a word from a Western language that could be used as an equivalent to Tao, perhaps the best choice would be 'The Ultimate'. There is nothing prior to the Tao.

> When the Tao had no name, that was the beginning of heaven and earth:
> Then, when it had a name, this was 'mother of all creation'.[7]

This verse makes clear the ultimacy of the Tao. It was before heaven and earth. It is therefore not just the cosmos or nature, but prior to them. Perhaps it is the 'mother of creation' that we might call 'nature'. Is the Tao then an immaterial reality, a spiritual reality? I do not think that would be an appropriate way of speaking. Our conception of 'spirit' is too vague for it to be used to explain some even more difficult concept. I think one can also say that the Tao is not a person and therefore not God, as that word is usually understood in the West. Yet this mysterious Tao which seems to hover between Being and non-being is invested with a power so ultimate that everything that is has its existence, might we venture to say, by the grace of the Tao.

Let us go back for a moment to look more carefully at the title of the book we are considering. It seems that at first it was, like many ancient Chinese books, simply called by the name of its putative author, the 'Lao-zu'. About the turn of the eras, it acquired its present name, *Tao Te Ching*. Translated quite literally, this title reads *Way Power Book*. As this English is too stark even for a newspaper headline, we could translate it as *Book on the Power of the Way*. The word '*te*' is usually translated 'power' or 'virtue' and the title emphasizes the point that however elusive the Tao may be, it is nevertheless power, the Greatest. The word '*ching*' is used of a classical text, the best-known example being the *I Ching* or *Book of Changes*, the oldest Chinese book, supposed to have been written about 1000 BCE. Our particular classic, the *Tao Te Ching*, is divided into two parts, of which the first deals mainly with the Tao and the second with the Te or the influence of the Tao in human life.

The book is sub-divided into brief chapters very loosely joined together and each chapter contains a number of sayings, again only loosely connected. Like the sayings in the Gospels, they have been compared to beads that have been strung together. Perhaps a better comparision would be with German textbooks on philosophy and theology. These were often written in numbered sections, and at the beginning of each section was printed a sentence or two summarizing the contents. Then followed a detailed discussion of the point made in the introductory sentence. A good example of this method of exposition is Schleiermacher's textbook of dogmatics, *The Christian Faith*. Sometimes the section headings were printed as 'outlines of dogmatics' without the explanatory material which constituted the bulk of the book. One could think of the *Tao Te Ching* as being rather like an outline. Ideas are placed before the reader, but he or she has to think out the explanation and enlargement of these ideas. That explains why this short book of 5000 characters is not like a short story to be read and comprehended at a sitting, but demands that each sentence be mulled over. After all the years since it was composed, people are still arguing about what it means.

We see something of this form and receive further help in understanding what the Tao is and what it is not from chapter 32:

> The Tao, considered as unchanging, has no name. Though in its primordial simplicity, it may be small, it is impossible to master it. If a king or prince could guard and hold it, all would spontaneously submit themselves to him. Heaven and earth [under its guidance] unite together and send down the sweet dew, which, without human interference, reaches equally in all directions of its own accord. As soon as it proceeds to action, it has a name. When it once has that name, people can learn to rest in it. When they learn to rest in it, they can be free from all risk of failure and error.

A great deal of the wisdom of the Tao can be gained from thinking over this brief paragraph. First, we are reminded of the very beginning of the book which spoke of the indefinability of the Tao, nameless, formless, without any distinguishable characteristics. In worldly terms, it seems to be nothing at all. Yet somehow concealed in this elusive Ultimate is the power that moves the world. If an earthly ruler could master this power, everything would be subject to him. Here we are glimpsing the power or virtue (Te) of the Tao. Next, the notion of emanation (or something like emanation) is mentioned. The Tao takes a name, it enters the realm of the historical and the phenomenal. In this form it becomes accessible to human beings, so that they can 'rest' in it, that is to say, live in accordance with it rather than trying to force it to obey their wills.

This is the doctrine of *wu-wei* or 'inaction' as it is sometimes called. It would be a mistake to think this means just doing nothing or submerging oneself in the contemplation of ultimate reality to the neglect of what is going on around us. Rather, it is submerging one's own selfish and limited desires and opinions so as to go with the Tao. In that sense it is 'resting', but it is so far from mere idleness that it is recommended as a mode of successful government. It is, if you like, a 'laid back' mode of government in which government interferes as little as possible with the people, so that they hardly realize that anyone is governing them at all! It is the opposite of the totalitarian state, which tries to control every act and even every thought of the citizen. It is the opposite also of busy bureaucracy and of the petty regulations and so-called 'political correctness' that affects even the democracies nowadays. Power is not exercised by forcing and bullying the citizens into conforming to the ruler's ideology, be it autocratic or liberal, but by giving them too the freedom to follow the Tao. In chapter 57, an imaginary ruler says:

> I will do nothing, and the people will be transformed of themselves; I will keep quiet, and the people will of themselves become correct; I will take no trouble about it, and the people will of themselves become rich; I will manifest no ambition, and the people will of themselves attain to the primitive simplicity.

Perhaps Lao-zu underestimated the mean streak in all human nature and perhaps his methods would hardly work in the fiercely competitive world of the late twentieth century. But there is undoubtedly something attractive and deeply spiritual in all this.

Since he held such views, it is hardly necessary to add that Lao-zu, like other great religious leaders, was against war. His opinions are expressed in chapters 30 and 31:

> He who would assist a ruler in harmony with the Tao will not assert his mastery in the kingdom by force of arms. Such a course is sure to meet with its proper return. Wherever an army has been stationed, briars and thorns spring up. In the sequence of great armies there are sure to be bad years.
>
> [But supposing in some circumstances a war has become unavoidable,] a skilful commander strikes a decisive blow, and stops. He does not dare [by continuing his operations] to assert and complete his mastery. He will strike the blow, but will be on

his guard against being vain or boastful or arrogant in consequence of it. He strikes it as a matter of necessity, but not from a
wish for mastery.

About the commander-in-chief of a victorious army, Lao-zu remarks, 'He who has killed multitudes of men should weep for them
with the bitterest grief; and the victor in battle has his place in the
ranks of the mourners.'

If we have some doubts about the wisdom of Lao-zu's doctrine of
wu-wei in the conduct of human affairs, perhaps we would be
sympathetic to it as an attitude toward nature. We have seen that
nature is a kind of emanation from the Tao. I suspect that Lao-zu
would not have been happy in the age of technology and the massive
disruption of nature which it has brought. It seems certain that he
would have been in the forefront of those who have sought to protect
the environment from destructive exploitation. Just as the Tao has
let nature be, so wisdom would counsel us to respect the natural
order. It might even be claimed that Taoism is a custom-made
philosophy for the environmentalist, for in the Taoist view, the
whole takes precedence over the parts and the human race should
not be considered in isolation from the cosmic or finally the
ontological totality within which it lives, moves and has its being.

Would Lao-zu have gone so far as to be a supporter of 'animal
rights', a very controversial topic? Perhaps he would. At any rate, a
disciple of his, Lieh-zu (*c.* 300 BCE) tells a story which is obviously
inspired by Lao-zu's philosophy and which is very sympathetic to the
nonhuman creation. A citizen was going on a long journey, and
before leaving gave a feast for a thousand guests with many dishes of
meats, fishes and fowl. By way of a grace, he made a somewhat
foolish speech: 'How kind Heaven is to the human race. It provides
the five grain crops and nourishes the fish and birds for us to enjoy
and use.'

The twelve-year old son of one of the guests stood up and replied:

My lord is wrong! All life is born in the same way that we are and
we are all of the same kind. One species is not nobler than another;
it is simply that the strongest and cleverest rule over the weaker
and more stupid. Things eat each other and are then eaten, but
they were not brought into being for this. To be sure, we take the
things which we can eat and consume them, but you cannot claim
that Heaven made them in the first place just for us to eat. After all,

mosquitoes and gnats bite our skin, tigers and wolves eat our flesh. Does this mean Heaven originally created us for the sake of the mosquitoes, gnats, tigers and wolves?[8]

Though one may not be prepared to accept everything in the Taoist attitude to nature, it must be at least admitted that this ancient philosophy has spoken on issues that are very much alive today.

I have several times mentioned that there is something like a doctrine of emanation in the teachings of Lao-zu. I have used the term 'emanation' because there is a resemblance to the teaching of Plotinus.[9] In his philosophy, the One is nameless, formless, impersonal (or possibly suprapersonal), without quality or quantity, neither in motion nor at rest . . . and one might go on saying it is neither this nor that. Yet it embraces within itself *in nuce*, may one say, everything that has ever or will ever come into existence. From the One there comes by emanation the Mind or *Nous*, which contains the intellectual forms, the archetypes of all finite entities. Now the utter mystery of the One is (so far as this is possible) made accessible by the intelligible world. This Plotinian teaching seems very much like the doctrine of the Tao. The Tao also is nameless and formless, but then it takes a name and becomes the 'mother' of all finite beings. This, as has been said above, is not far from what we understand as 'nature'. But neither for Plotinus nor Lao-zu was nature or the material cosmos the ultimate reality, as it was for Stoics like Strato or for nineteenth-century materialists. Beyond the material universe lay, they believed, this impalpable indescribable reality, the One or the Tao.

In both Lao-zu and Plotinus, the process of emanation goes on. We are concerned here only with Lao-zu. In his way of expressing it (chapter 42):

> The Tao produced One; One produced Two; Two produced Three; Three produced all things. All things leave behind them the obscurity out of which they have come and go forward to embrace the brightness into which they have emerged, while they are harmonized by the breath of vacancy.

This is only a bare schema, but the One, the Two and the Three are filled out in the course of the book. The One (and we must note that Lao-zu means something quite different from Plotinus in his use of the expression) is the Tao that can be named, not the ultimate and nameless Tao. The Tao that is named is nature, or the cosmos, and because naming is possible, there is the possibility of understanding. The One, in turn, gives birth to the Two. The two are that celebrated pair, the yin and the yang. These are opposites, and they run through everything. They are exemplified in male and female, hot and cold, dry and moist and so on. The world process is a never-ending struggle between these opposites. But this is not a dualistic metaphysic, for yin never conquers yang nor yang yin. Rather, they exist in balance, each needing the other and holding the other in check. This notion of the struggle of opposites is common to many philosophies. Heraclitus taught it in ancient Greece, and it was still there in the Hegelian dialectic. I have mentioned elsewhere that one of the Chinese words for 'peace' is *ping*, which in its verbal use means 'adjust', 'harmonize', 'weigh in the balance', and 'here the idea seems to be a diversity in unity, or the taking up of the conflict into a kind of equilibrium of forces'.[10] This does seem to be a valuable idea. Peace is not something static, but a process toward an inclusive relationship, just as the conflict of yin and yang are embraced within the unity of the One. The Two, in turn, produce the Three. The Three are Heaven, Earth and the human race, represented by the ruler in the following quotation (chapter 25):

> The Ruler follows the Earth,
> Earth follows Heaven,
> Heaven follows the Tao,
> The Tao follows the law of its own Being.

'Heaven' (Tian) was one of the words used in Chinese for God. Does it mean 'God' here? Perhaps it does, but if so, it reinforces the point made above that the Tao is more ultimate even than God, a kind of 'God beyond God.

This metaphysical scheme of the Tao, then the One, then the yin and the yang, then the Three comprising Heaven, Earth and Man, and lastly 'all things' that flow from that trinity, is so different from Western metaphysical systems that it is hard for Western minds to adjust to it. Even its terminology is not quite consistent, but it has to be seen within the context of Lao-zu's total picture.

Like most of our mediators, Lao-zu was not himself a founder. Ideas like yin and yang and even Tao itself had already had a long history in Chinese thought, but undoubtedly it required someone of genius to build out of that miscellany of ideas a metaphysical, ethical and political vision that can still stretch our minds and challenge our unthinking prejudices.

The office of mediator would not have seemed strange to Lao-zu. Martin Palmer has pointed out that the early religion of China was a form of Shamanism which at one time was spread through much of northern and eastern Asia. The shaman was an ecstatic figure, a kind of mystic who could communicate with the unseen world and could also bring healing and other blessings to human beings. The Emperor of China himself was a kind of mediator who at the appropriate times offered sacrifices to Heaven on behalf of the people and thereby secured for them various benefits.[11]

Lao-zu drew on that heritage and purified and enriched it beyond measure. Unfortunately, in course of time his teachings were sadly reduced to the level of superstitions and infiltrated by self-interest on the part of the believers searching for longevity, immortality and material blessings. But one wonders if a doctrine so difficult to understand could ever have become a religion for the people without falling into corruption. Juang-zu declares: 'The Tao that is made clear is not the Tao.'[12] Of course, Augustine said something very similar about the God of Christian faith. I hope I have not made the Tao too clear, and I feel so unclear about it in my own mind that I do not think I have offended. But I am clear, as I said above, that some of Lao-zu's insights are directly relevant to the problems of our own times, and I am happy to hear that the faith of this old mediator is currently reviving and reforming itself.

4

Buddha

(563–483 BCE)

Buddha and Buddhism arose out of the ancient tradition of Indian religion, and took over many things from that tradition, especially the doctrine of *samsara* according to which the soul of a deceased person migrates at death into a new body, and the doctrine of *karma* which teaches that each new existence is determined by the good or evil done in former existences. The word 'buddha' is derived from the Sanskrit *budh*, the root of a verb which means 'to awaken', 'to perceive' or 'to know'. A buddha is one who has been awakened or, as it is often translated, enlightened. He is like one who has awakened from sleep and is able to distinguish reality from dreams. The religion of Buddhism stresses thought, meditation, understanding, intellect, but not when these are misdirected into idle speculation, for Buddhism is at the same time very practical and is a way of life and of salvation.

'Buddha' is a title, not a proper name. According to Buddhist teaching, there have been and will be many buddhas. Periodically, a Buddha will come to earth to preach enlightenment; also, all the faithful in Buddhism have entered on the way to enlightenment and aspire to become buddhas. There is a parallel usage in Christianity, where 'Christ' is not a proper name but a title, meaning an 'anointed one', or in Hebrew a 'messiah'. Some theologians, notably Origen and Luther, sometimes spoke of all Christians as 'christs'. But just as Jesus is often called simply Christ, the title having been converted into a proper name, so the title Buddha has become virtually the name of the most famous among the buddhas. He must be counted as one who is a mediator and to whom many millions of human beings, especially but not exclusively in Asia, look up as to a saviour. When Buddha is mentioned in this chapter, the reference is to this particular individual, unless the context makes clear that the term is being used in a more general sense.

As with the other mediators in this study, the first thing to be said about Buddha is that he was a human being like the rest of us. This has to be asserted, for like the other mediators, his humanity has been covered up under layers of legend. Tradition claims that he was born around the year 563 BCE[1] near a city then called Kapilavastu in Nepal. He was given the personal name Siddhartha, and his family name was Gautama. His father was *raja* or ruler of a state in that part of the world. But even Buddha's birth has been mythologized, and he is said to have descended from one of the Buddhist heavens into his mother's womb, already fully aware of his identity and his vocation. It should be said here, however, that the various myths and legends that attached to Buddha are not to be simply swept aside. Although they do not possess literal truth, they are frequently ways of expressing profound truths of the Buddhist faith, and this will become clear to us as we go along.

As a ruler, Buddha's father or putative father belonged to the aristocratic warrior caste, the *kshatriya* caste. No doubt he hoped that his son would follow him as ruler. But soon after the child's birth – so runs the legend – a sage named Asita came to see him and prophesied that if he remained at home he would become a great ruler, but if he left home to become a wandering ascetic, he would become a fully enlightened buddha. The father was worried by this prophecy and tried to ensure that the child would be brought up in such a way that he would cling to the comforts and advantages of his station and not be diverted into the life of religion.

But what the father feared eventually came to pass. Probably the plain unvarnished story was that the sensitive and thoughtful youngster saw much of the pain and misery of life in the rural area where he lived and was deeply affected by what he saw. On the other hand, he found no satisfaction in the delights with which his father sought to divert him. This sober version of his development may well be the correct one[2] but the tendency to legend has left us an account which is so well-known and so closely tied in with our understanding of Buddha that it cannot be omitted. However, this is what I would call 'true legend', in the sense that while it is not factual history, it has dramatized the events of Buddha's development in such a way as to bring what must have been a remarkable story to more vivid expression than would have been possible by a sober account of the young man's internal broodings. In any case, we have no access to these. Here then is the story. I have somewhat abridged it, as the original is verbose and repetitious by Western standards. Our mediator is called in this passage the Bodhisattva, that is, one destined to be a Buddha. Strictly speaking, he becomes Buddha only after his enlightenment:

> Now one day the Bodhisattva, wishing to go to the park, summoned his charioteer and asked him to harness the chariot. He obeyed, and adorning the great splendid chariot with all its adornments yoked the four state horses white as lotus petals, and informed the Bodhisattva. The Bodhisattva ascended the chariot, which was like a vehicle of the gods, and went towards the park. The gods thought: 'The time for Prince Siddhartha to attain enlightenment is at hand: we shall show him a previous sign.' So they made a god appear, worn out with old age, with broken teeth, grey hair, bent, with broken-down body, a stick in hand, and trembling. The Bodhisattva asked his charioteer, 'What man is this? Even his hair is not like that of others.' [The charioteer said, 'Everyone who is born and lives long enough inevitably comes to old age.'] Hearing this reply, the Bodhisattva said, 'Woe to birth, when we see the old age of all that are born.' With agitated heart, he thereupon returned and went up to his palace. The king asked why his son had returned so quickly. 'O king, he has seen an old man, and on seeing an old man, he will leave the world.'[3] 'By this you are ruining me. Get together dancing girls for my son. If he enjoys luxury, he will have no thought of leaving the world'.[4]

This little story of an excursion to the park is repeated three times in almost identical words. On the second excursion, the Bodhisattva sees a sick person, on the third he meets a corpse, and on both occasions he again hurries home, deeply upset and depressed by these unhappy sights. He makes a fourth excursion, and this time they meet a man who had abandoned the world and taken up the life of an ascetic. His charioteer explained, and commended the life of renunciation. On the same day, the Bodhisattva resolved to leave the world at midnight – the incident which Buddhists call 'the great renunciation'. So at midnight he left the city, having taken leave of his wife and young son. At the city gate, he was encountered by the tempter, Mara, who promised him rule over a vast empire if only he would turn back – an incident which prompts comparison with Satan's temptation of Jesus in the New Testament. But the Bodhisattva's mind was made up and he went his way. Mara, for his part, decided to dog the Bodhisattva's footsteps and to plague him continually with temptations. The Bodhisattva is said to have been twenty-nine years of age when he made his great renunciation.

A period of about six years intervened, while he sought enlightenment. First he went to two religious teachers, and hoped that he might learn from them. Apparently he did learn something of the technique of meditation, but his experience was on the whole disappointing. Next he practised the most severe austerities. I pass over the details, probably exaggerated, of this period of asceticism, which seems to have reduced him to a physical wreck, but did not bring the peace of mind for which he was searching. Eventually he decided to abandon the path of asceticism and he once again began to take a reasonable amount of food and drink. Was there another and better path to enlightenment? He remembered how, as a boy, he had once sat under a tree on his father's estate, and without the rigours of asceticism but rather through a mental discipline had attained to a state of trance. Was that the way he should follow now?

So the story goes on to the enlightenment, the Bodhisattva now being about thirty-five. According to the tradition, he again sat under a tree, called the bodhi-tree or enlightenment-tree. During the three watches of the night he went through four stages of trance, in which desires and evil ideas are overcome, and a serene equanimity is attained. In the first watch, he thought of the many former existences through which he had come. In the second watch, he thought of *karma*, the chain of causation that runs through these existences, evil bringing misery in rebirth, good leading to a higher state of being. In the third watch he directed his mind to the destruction of the *asavas*, that is to say, sensual desires, desire for existence, ignorance. He realized the pain of birth and rebirth, the cause of that pain, that is, desire, and the way to the cessation of pain, that is, the extinction of desire. In the words attributed to Buddha himself,

> I realized that destroyed is rebirth, the religious life has been led, done is what was to be done, there is nothing for me beyond this world.[5] This was the third knowledge that I gained in the last watch of the night. Ignorance was dispelled, knowledge arose. Darkness was dispelled, light arose. So it is with him who abides vigilant, strenuous and resolute.[6]

So the Bodhisattva had now attained the status of a fully enlightened Buddha. But Mara is hard on his heels. Having achieved enlightenment, Buddha is tempted to stop at that point. Must he now go on and preach the doctrine to people who are unwilling to hear it?

Through painful striving have I gained it.
Away with now proclaiming it!
By those beset by lust and hate
Not easily is this doctrine learned.

But he resists the temptation to inaction. He thinks of the mass of humanity sunk in suffering and ignorance. He himself was now an *arahat*, a non-returner who would go to *nirvana* at death and for whom there would be no more rebirth. So he recognizes his obligation to pass on what he has learned. He remembers that when he was practising his austerities at an earlier stage of his search, five disciples had borne him company. When he left off his self-mortification and began to eat and drink again, these disciples had left him, believing that he had given up his quest. Buddha learned that they were now in the neighbourhood of Benares, so he set off for that city intending to begin his preaching with these former disciples. Perhaps they would be more responsive to his teaching than people with whom he had no previous acquaintance.

So to them he preached his first sermon. Whether in fact he preached the sermon in the terms in which it has been preserved is doubtful, but as E. J. Thomas has said, it 'certainly contains the fundamental principles of Buddhism'.[7] It proclaims Buddhism as a middle way between a life dominated by the passions and a life given over to painful asceticism. It also contains the basic teaching of the Four Noble Truths and the Noble Eightfold Path. I quote it in a slightly abridged form:

This, O monks, is the middle way. (1) This is the noble truth of pain; birth is painful, old age is painful, sickness is painful, death is painful, sorrow, lamentation, dejection and despair are painful. Contact with unpleasant things is painful, not getting what one wants is painful. (2) This, O monks, is the noble truth of the cause of pain: that craving, which leads to rebirth, combined with pleasure and lust, finding pleasure here and there, the craving for passion, the craving for existence, the craving for non-existence. (3) This, O monks, is the noble truth of the cessation of pain: the cessation without a remainder of that craving; abandonment, forsaking, release, non-attachment. (4) This, O monks, is the noble truth of the way that leads to the cessation of pain: this is the noble eightfold path, namely, right views, right intention, right speech, right action, right livelihood, right effort, right mindfulness, right concentration. Thus, O monks among doctrines unheard of before, by me was this truth comprehended, in me sight and knowledge arose.[8]

This first sermon may indeed contain the basic truths of Buddha's teaching, but it is so brief and therefore so basic that we would like to know something more. The first three of the Four Noble Truths are perhaps sufficiently plain, but we need more light on the fourth, the one which sets out the eightfold path. What exactly do these various items – right views, right intention, right speech, and so on – mean? Concerning the Four Noble Truths and the Noble Eightfold Path, Christmas Humphreys remarks, 'Basic though these teachings are in every school of Buddhism, it is not easy to display them at best advantage from any single passage in the scriptures.'[9] He then goes on to quote a modern exposition of these basic truths, itself drawn from the Buddhist scriptures, but giving more details than are found in the first sermon. This exposition is too long to quote in full here, and I content myself with a summary of the part which deals with the eightfold path. That eightfold path lies at the very centre of Buddha's teaching and lifestyle. It explains the mental discipline which Buddha commended as a 'middle way' between the life of passion and the life of self-mortification. Let us then inquire more closely into each of the eight items mentioned as belonging to the path. Different translators have varied in their renderings of some of the words. In what follows, I have standardized these translations to conform with the version of the first sermon given above.

'Right views' is the first item in the eightfold path. It would seem to indicate simply the Four Noble Truths themselves. The person who holds these truths has a right view or right understanding of good and evil. It is not necessary that a person should understand whether the world is temporal or eternal, finite or infinite, what existence if any one will have after death. Thus although 'right views' stand at the beginning of the path and give it an intellectual slant, it is not necessary to get into abstruse metaphysical questions in order to live the good life.

'Right intention' stands next on the list, but 'intention' is an ambiguous term. In the version publicized by Humphreys, three things are needed for a right intention: thought free from sensuality, thought free from ill-will, thought free from cruelty.

What is 'right speech'? The person who has right speech abstains from lying and falsehood, even when it might seem to be to his disadvantage. He abstains also from slander, abuse, harsh language and vain talk. The aim of his talking is to spread concord by his words. 'There are two things to which one should adhere; either conversation about the truth, or holy silence.'

Next is 'right action'. Negatively, this means that one abstains from killing, stealing and unlawful sexual intercourse. Affirmatively, it means that one is compassionate and cherishes kindness and pity for all living beings.

Then there is 'right livelihood'. This means that one earns a living by an honourable occupation. There is no attempt to list all the honourable occupations, but five occupations are named as forbidden to a Buddhist: trading in arms, trading in living beings (including, one may suppose, animals as well as slaves), trading in flesh, trading in intoxicating drinks and trading in poison.

'Right effort' means exercising one's energy to avoid temptation and to overcome evil if temptations do arise.

'Right mindfulness' means giving heed to what is going on in one's existence, contemplation of the body and awareness of its states, of the sensations, of the mind and of internal phenomena. This fourfold contemplation is essential to entering on and pursuing the right path.

Finally, 'Right concentration', which demands both right effort and right mindfulness, keeps the disciple fixed on the goal of attaining the status of an *arahat*.[10]

Here we seem to be grappling with the basic concepts of Buddhism in a form which may not be very far from the Master's own teaching. What may strike someone from another tradition is that this basic Buddhism is very much a 'do it yourself' version of salvation. This, of course, may be a wrong impression. Certainly there are later forms of Buddhism which acknowledge something like grace and divine assistance in the quest for salvation, and perhaps these developments would not have come about unless there had already been some seed present at the origin. These are questions that will have to be faced later in this chapter. But before we ask whether, for instance, Buddhism is atheistic, or whether, in spite of its religious origins, it is really a humanism, we should consider further some of the early teaching. We find it in that famous discourse, the *Dhammapada*

('Path of Virtue') which many scholars believe to be a fairly reliable account of the Buddha's own teaching.[11]

The *Dhammapada* is not a unitary treatise but a collection of 423 utterances on moral and religious topics. The name, as has been indicated, means 'path of virtue' and it presupposes the eightfold path, specifically mentioned in verse 191. But the *Dhammapada* is not schematically divided according to the eight points mentioned in the eightfold path, so in presenting the *Dhammapada*, I have selected what seems to me to be some of the most significant verses and have grouped them according to their topics so that we can see their bearing on the questions we have still to ask, about whether Buddha's teaching is atheistic, what is the nature of the self in his thought, what is *nirvana*. The actual groups will be as follows: (1) Sayings of the Buddha which invite comparison with sayings of other mediators, including Jesus Christ. (2) Sayings about the human self and its destiny. (3) Sayings about the Buddha himself in relation to gods and men. (4) Sayings about God, gods and ultimate reality. The numbers of the verses quoted are shown in brackets.

The following sayings show the ethical convergence of the great religions, and each of them has parallels among other mediators. On love and hatred: 'Hatred does not cease by hatred at any time; hatred ceases by love' [5]. On the need for a fundamental decision in life: 'One is the road that leads to wealth, another the road that leads to *nirvana*' [75]. On the human tendency to ignore death: 'Death carries off a man who is gathering flowers [spending his life in pleasures] and whose mind is distracted, as a flood carries off a sleeping village' [47]; also, '"These sons belong to me and this wealth". With such thoughts a fool is tormented. He does not belong to himself, how much less sons and wealth?' [62]. On the futility of self-mortification: 'Not nakedness, not platted hair, not dirt, not fasting or lying on the earth, not rubbing with dust, not sitting motionless, can purify a mortal who has not overcome desires' [141]. On the tendency to blame and criticize other people: 'Not the failures of others, not their sins of commission and omission should the wise man blame, but his own misdeeds and negligences' [50]. The message of the enlightened one: 'Not to commit any sin, to do good and to purify one's mind, that is the teaching of the Buddha' [183].

The foregoing very brief selection of verses from the *Dhammapada* makes it clear that the aspirations of the Buddha resemble in many respects those of the leaders of other world religions and are expressed with clarity and often with elegance. They entitle both Buddha himself and the multitudes who have followed him (to the extent that they have lived up to their profession) to our deepest respect. But we must now go on and look at passages touching on those aspects of Buddha's teaching which are unclear or which may seem to have a dubious spiritual value. And first we consider the teaching about the human self and its destiny.

'All that we are is the result of what we have thought: it is founded on our thoughts, it is made up of our thoughts. If a man speaks or acts with an evil thought, pain follows him . . . if he speaks or acts with a pure thought, happiness follows him' [1, 2]. One may wonder whether the stress on the inner life (the exercise of 'right mindfulness') is not too introspective and perhaps ties one to self-centredness. Here we meet again the strong emphasis on thought and the intellectual character of Buddhism, though this same quotation makes it clear that thought is closely connected with speech and action. The thought intended here is not the thought that wanders off into speculation about possibly unanswerable questions, but the thought that contributes to the being and activity of the complete person. Another point to be noted here is that Buddha, like the other mediators, is not an innovator beginning from scratch. He takes over various items from the Indian tradition of religion and spirituality, just as he rejects other items from that tradition. In the quotations just made, he is clearly accepting the traditional doctrines of *samsara* and *karma*, that is to say, that after death the soul is reborn in a new body, and that the nature of the rebirth is determined by the good or evil done in the former existence.

There is much more about the self in the *Dhammapada*. Very important is the idea of mastering one's own self. 'If one man conquers in battle a million men, and if another conquers himself, it is the latter who is the greatest of conquerors' [103]. 'Self is the lord of self, who else could be the lord? With self well subdued, a man finds a lord such as few can find' [160]. 'Self is the lord of self, self is the refuge of self, therefore curb thyself as merchants curb a good horse' [380]. What is the understanding of self in these verses? Who or what is this self that can become lord over the self? Buddha must have in mind what in Western philosophy we might express by saying that the self has a relation to itself. Does it then become another self or a second self? No, but it reveals the complexity of the self. The self can become an object to itself, yet in that very act it remains a subject, and the subject *qua* subject can never be objectified. I can play chess, I can think of myself playing chess, I can be angry with myself for playing so stupidly, but the subject-self keeps retreating before the process of objectification and is never caught in the process.

These points have to be borne in mind when we consider another item in Buddha's teaching, the doctrine of *anatta* or no-self. This is sometimes interpreted with Western presuppositions as if it were the equivalent of Hume's teaching that there is no abiding self but simply the succession of changing contents of consciousness. If one pushes this interpretation, then Buddhism begins to appear as a kind of nihilism. But such an interpretation seems inconsistent with the language about the self mastering self or indeed with the whole motivation of Buddha's quest which was the quest for some kind of fulfilment. This does not, I think, depend on the existence of a substantial soul, but it does presuppose a unitary self of some description persisting through the successive experiences.

Nevertheless, the suspicion that Buddhism may in the end be both atheistic and nihilistic is not to be lightly dismissed. It gets further support from the fact that *nirvana* (in Pali, *nibbana*) means 'extinguishing', as in putting out a fire or a light. But one might argue that what is extinguished is desire, greed, anger and whatever else makes human life evil and sorrowful. This question of an alleged Buddhist nihilism was examined by Max Müller.[12] He agrees that it would be surprising if Buddha taught that the human being must strive through all the phases of existence toward *nirvana* only to fall into nothingness. But he also agrees that the Buddhist scholastics did think that the Buddhist *summum bonum* or *nirvana* is the absolute nothing. The 'scholastics' were the authors of the third part or 'Basket' of the Buddhist canonical scriptures called the *Tripitaka* (Three Baskets). But he holds that this scholastic teaching is inconsistent with the teaching in the first two 'baskets'. It is in the first two parts of the canon (the parts on which the expositions given in this chapter have been based) that we are most likely to have the teaching of Buddha himself, though of course one can never be sure in any of the great religions where the teaching of the leader merges into the teaching of the disciples. But I think that one can be fairly certain that Buddha's own teaching was a message of hope, not of nihilism. What, for instance, do we make of his promise, 'Those who, when the law has been well preached to them, follow the law, will pass across the dominion of death, however difficult to overcome' [86]? So even if it is the case that in the so-called *Abhidarma* or scholastic portion of the *Tripitaka* there is something close to a nihilism, this was not the message of the mediator himself. There may be further evidence for this in the fact that later developments in Buddhism, in the Mahayana schools of thought, introduced notions of *nirvana* as a kind of paradise or 'Pure Land', though such ideas may also have been far from the austere thinking of Buddha. He would surely have said that *nirvana* is indescribable and would probably have discouraged imaginative efforts to picture it.

How did the Buddha understand himself? Some passages in the canon may disturb us. In the aftermath of the enlightenment, He declares:

Victorious over all, omniscient am I,
In all things of the world free from defilement;
Leaving all, with craving gone, emancipated,
And knowledge all self-gained, whom should I follow?

Instructor, teacher, have I none,
One like me is nowhere to be found;
In the world with its gods and men
No one is there to rival me.

In a teacher who has proclaimed the doctrine of no-self, this sounds very egotistical! We may suppose, however, that the words have been placed in his mouth by a zealous disciple. We may compare utterances attributed to Jesus in John's Gospel, such as 'Before Abraham was, I am', or 'I am the way, the truth and the life'. A commentator would explain these by saying that in this Gospel, the utterances are not those of the human Jesus but of the divine Logos which was incarnate in Jesus. Similarly in this Buddhist text, we should not think that the human historical Buddha, Siddartha Gautama, is claiming to be superior to both gods and men. The point is that the principle he embodies (I shall come back to explain this expression) is something ultimate, beyond either the human or the divine realms. In this sense, he is god beyond gods (*devatideva*).

What about the gods, then? Did Buddha recognize them? This raises the question of his alleged atheism. Buddha was certainly not an atheist in the sense that he denied the gods of India. Just as he accepted *samsara* and *karma*, so he accepted the Hindu pantheon.

But he does seem to have deprived the gods of any importance. We have seen that his scheme of salvation was something that he worked out for himself. Anything like grace or divine assistance appears to have been superfluous. What seems also to be true is that he did not think of the gods as creators either of the universe or of the human race. Though the world of the gods might endure for millions of years, it would eventually come to an end in the cycle of the ages when a new era would begin. In a verse of the *Dhammapada* [153] he does speak of 'the maker of this tabernacle', apparently referring to his own body, but the saying is obscure, and his real opinion seems to be stated in a discourse where the Hindu creator-god, Brahma, is the first to awaken in a new world-age, and then when he sees other beings around him, he supposes that he has created them.

But does Buddha believe in a reality more ultimate than the gods, a Godhead beyond God, so to speak? Probably he does. When I mentioned above the bold words in which Buddha seemed to declare himself superior even to gods, I said this was because of the supreme principle which he embodied, not something that was personal to him as Siddhartha Gautama. The idea was elaborated by Buddhist theologians as the doctrine of the three bodies of the Buddha. One is the phenomenal body, the body of the actual human being who lived in the sixth century BCE. We all have a picture of this body, which has been represented again and again in Asian art, and is still to be seen in sculptures and pictures all over the Buddhist world. He also had a heavenly body in his preterrestial life. But beyond them all is his body without form, unimaginable, unpicturable. It is called the *Dharmakaya* and is the ultimate cosmic principle. If the word 'God' must be expressed in personal terms, then Buddha might be called an atheist. But if God can also mean the ultimate or the absolute or Holy Being, conceived as impersonal or suprapersonal, then Buddha too has a God and mediates that God to those who follow in his 'path of virtue'. The *Dharmakaya* may be compared to the One of Plotinus, the 'God beyond God' of some Christian mystics, and the Tao of Lao-zu. And just as Christianity teaches that we may see the form of Christ in every human being because each one is made in the image of God, so Buddhism claims that everyone has a 'Buddha within' and has the potentiality of attaining to buddhahood.[13]

We broke off our narration of the Buddha's career after his first sermon in order to give an account of the teaching which he felt himself summoned to impart to his fellow human beings. He gave that teaching over many years and founded a community which has since then grown to be one of the major religions of the world. He died in 483 BCE at the age of eighty, and, we hope, attained his goal. Some sentences from the *Dhammapada* may sum up the chapter:

Men, driven by fear, go to many a refuge, to mountains and forests, to groves and sacred trees. But that is not a safe refuge, that is not the best refuge; a man is not delivered from all pains after going to that refuge. He who takes refuge with Buddha, the law, and the community; he who with clear understanding sees the four holy truths, namely, pain, the origin of pain, the destruction of pain, and the eightfold holy way that leads to the quieting of pain – that is the safe refuge, that is the best refuge; having gone to that refuge, a man is delivered from all pain [188–92].

5

Confucius

(551–479 BCE)

In our chapter on Lao-zu, it was noted that China, perhaps because of its large population and long history, has produced two great mediators, Lao-zu and Confucius. The name Confucius is a latinization of his Chinese name, Kung-fu-zu, or simply Kung-zu. Just as Lao-zu was not a founder but one who built on the long tradition of Chinese thought and religion, so Confucius drew upon the same tradition. He said himself, 'I am a transmitter and not an innovator. I believe in and have a passion for the ancients'.[1] Of course, to point to the dependence of both of these men on the tradition is not to deny that they had originality. They brought new understandings and developments to the tradition, and this is evidenced by the fact that out of that tradition they produced very differing bodies of teaching. We have seen that Lao-zu gave a central place to the mystical and metaphysical doctrine of the Tao, though he also derived some practical consequences from his speculations. Confucius on the contrary showed a certain impatience with speculative questions, and concentrated on ethics and politics. His teaching, on the whole, was pragmatic, humanist and this-worldly. If this is the case, should we include him in this study of mediators? I think that the justification for doing so is that there are many types of religions, some contemplative and quietist, others intensely practical, with many variations between the extremes. Confucius was certainly a religious man, as we shall see, but he believed that religion must issue in conduct, and he carried this to the point where religion becomes a background, and attention is focussed on moral and practical questions, not only in the lives of individuals but in the broader sphere of society. Although later Confucianism probably departed quite far from Confucius' own teaching and became a kind of 'civic religion', some people might argue that a religion ought to become an overtly formative influence in society and not be content to inspire only individual devotion and righteousness, but only later shall we be able to form a judgment on the place of Confucius among the mediators.

Confucius was born probably in 551 BCE in the city of Tsou in the state of Lu, now part of the province of Shantung. China was at that time in a chaotic condition. There was no central government for the whole country, but a large number of small states, engaged in almost constant warfare with one another. Each state had its own ruler, usually possessed of despotic power, but even within the states there was little in the way of central government, for the ruler was frequently rendered impotent by powerful nobles and warlords who were out to seize power, rather like the feudal barons of mediaeval Europe. In that situation, the common people were the worst sufferers. Confucius must have been a sensitive youth, for he was deeply aware of this suffering all around him. His experience at this point is comparable to that of the young Buddha. But whereas Buddha looked for a way by which individuals might escape by rising above the situation by meditation and attaining a personal salvation, Confucius looked for a bolder remedy. Was there a possibility of changing the society itself? Is the natural condition of the human race one of war, in which ruler struggles against other rulers, and every ruler struggles against his own subject people, exacting from them the maximum in taxes, forced labour and military service, or is the natural condition one in which these adversarial relationships are done away and replaced by co-operation, both among rulers and as between rulers and people? These questions remind us of the different points of view of Hobbes and Locke in seventeenth-century England. Hobbes believed that the natural state of mankind is one of war. Locke – like Confucius – believed that the state of nature is that of 'men living together according to reason'.[2] Admittedly, this teaching takes an optimistic view of human nature, and there is much in history and experience that might incline us to a pessimistic view. But one has also to admit that if the pessimistic view is the correct one, there is little hope for the future of humanity.

We do not know how Confucius arrived at his beliefs or how he managed to aquire an education. But somehow he did both. It may have been the case that his family was one of many families of the minor nobility that had been evicted and impoverished in those stormy times. He says of himself: 'I was of humble station when young. That is why I am skilled in many menial things.'[3] There is surely a touch of humour and certainly no bitterness in this saying. It does seem clear, however, that from his youth he devoted himself to learning, and went on from learning to teaching. He thus summarized his own career: 'At fifteen, I set my heart on learning. At thirty, I took my stand. At forty, I had no doubts. At fifty, I understood the decrees of Heaven. At sixty, my ear was obedient [to their call]. At seventy, I followed my heart's desire, for I did not overstep the boundaries of right.'[4] But we can only understand this summary when we have seen the rest of Confucius' career and can fill in the gaps.

Most of what we know about Confucius comes from the book *Lun yu*, known in English as *The Analects*. It consists of short passages usually of exchanges between Confucius and his students, sometimes in the setting of some incident. It is believed that at least the first half of this book goes back near enough to Confucius' time as to give us reasonable confidence that it preserves genuine teaching of his. The records of the historian Si-ma Qien (quoted above in the chapter on Lao-zu) are suspect by many critics, including the story of the meeting between the two masters, Lao and Kung. Even less reliable are the stories that come from later Confucianism. Some of them are obviously legendary. For instance, there is the almost stock legend which seems to crop up with all our mediators – the legend of supernatural events at the birth; in the case of Confucius, dragons and spirits hovering in the air. Confucius, perhaps because he himself played down the supernatural, usually comes across as an unmistakably human figure, but even his human status becomes threatened, especially after the emperor began to make sacrifices to Confucius. This practice began in 59 CE, and was still continuing in the middle of the twentieth century, just before the communists came to power in China. Of course, we should remember that prayers and sacrifices to ancestors is an age-old custom in China and we should not read too much into it. A further difficulty in getting authentic information about Confucius arises from the fact that long after his lifetime, when there was rivalry between Confucianism and other philosophies, some of the adherents of these other philosophies inserted their own doctrines into the Confucian books, including *The Analects*. Just to make things really difficult, the first Emperor, who unified the country after the chaotic period of the warring states, ordered the wholesale burning of Confucian books, and had four hundred and sixty Confucian scholars buried alive. So even this cool civilized religion did not escape persecution.

We have seen that Confucius entertained the dream of a renewed Chinese society in which rulers and people would co-operate for the good of all. It seems that for a long time he hoped that the ruler of Lu might appoint him to a ministerial post in which he would be able to work toward the transformation he desired. He may have held minor posts, but it is more likely that he had to work as a free-lance teacher and it was in teaching and scholarship that he found satisfaction. His method of teaching was not by lectures, but by what we would now call 'seminars' when he would discuss a topic with a small group, or even in individual tutorials. He was able to have many of his students placed in responsible positions in the public service. He may have hoped to accomplish through them what he had been unable to do himself. When we read *The Analects*, we get the impression that he enjoyed a very good relation with most of his students. As a true lover of learning himself, he urged them to engage in study for its own sake, and not for the salary which it might bring. This was only one item in a wider moral principle he taught, that the reward of virtue lies in the virtuous act itself, not in any extrinsic recompense.

When Confucius was over fifty, he was at last offered what appeared to be an important appointment in the Lu administration. Already some of his own students were occupying responsible positions. It looked as if Confucius would at last get his chance to put his ideas into practice. But it did not turn out like that. The appointment offered him had a certain honorific status, but with no real power attached. Confucius had to recognize that his plans for reforming society were not going to get anywhere, at least, not under his direction. The state of Lu had no use for him. In frustration, he decided to leave Lu to its own devices, and set out on a journey through the neighbouring states. There he spent longer or shorter periods with various rulers, advising them on their problems. He spent about twelve years in this wandering life, and then about 484 BCE he was invited back to Lu. But Confucius was now sixty-seven. When he got back, he resumed his teaching, but his dream of ever playing an active part in public affairs had faded. Perhaps that was just as well, for his talents lay in teaching and scholarship, and it cannot be said that he would have been successful in the realm of public affairs – though, as he was never given the chance it cannot be said either that he would have been unsuccessful. He died in 479 and it is said that his disciples mourned near his grave for three years.

What then were the teachings of this man who was so revered by his disciples, and who, though spurned by the rulers of his day, stamped his influence so effectively, not only on Chinese politics but on the entire culture, that it remains to the present day?

The fundamental conception is Tao, literally 'the way'. We have already met the word Tao in Lao-zu, and it had been used in Chinese thinking before his time. But Confucius gives it a quite different meaning from the one it bears in the *Tao Te Ching*. In that book, Tao is the final ontological reality, the mysterious source from which everything that is arises. In Confucius, Tao is an ethical or practical conception. It has been compared to 'natural law' in Western philosophy, but if the comparison with natural law seems too abstract or too general, a closer comparison might be with the way (*hodos*) as the expression is used in the Acts of the Apostles (9. 2, etc.). There it is used in a concrete sense for the nascent Christian movement and all it embodied. Similarly Confucius speaks of 'the way' for the way of life which he taught, though he obviously thinks it is a way for all mankind and one which could be constructed from a study of human nature itself. In so far as it can be derived from human nature, then it resembles 'natural law' as taught by St Thomas Aquinas and many others. This way holds for individuals, but also for society and perhaps for the universe – and when one mentions the universe, then something like a metaphysical note comes in, and with it a relation between the Confucian and Taoist conceptions of Tao. There is another saying which introduces a religious relation to the Tao, and is very close to what an Israelite might have said about the law of the Lord. It is quoted by Creel, who remarks: 'Mere intellectual acquiescence in the Way was by no means enough. "Those who merely know it", Confucius said, "are not equal to those who love it; and those who love it are not equal to those who delight in it".'[5]

We have seen that the way could be considered as a kind of 'natural law', deriving its content from human nature itself. So our next step is to ask how Confucius understood human nature and how far 'the way' can be judged to lead to the fulfilment of that nature. Confucius seems to have believed in the natural goodness of the human being. This may be due to a kind of native optimism in the

Chinese character, for we remember that Lao-zu, despite his many differences from Confucius, also believed that if people are left to themselves and freed from governmental interference, they will go along with the Tao, and that would be something like following the way in a Confucian sense.[6] According to D.C. Lau, Confucius' 'unquestioned assumption' was that 'the only purpose a man can have and the only worthwhile thing a man can do is to become as good a man as possible'.[7] This belief in the inherent goodness of human beings was carried even further by Confucius' greatest follower, Mencius,[8] who lived about two centuries after Confucius and whose enthusiasm for Confucius' teaching earned for him the title of the 'Second Sage'. Mencius claimed that it is as natural for man to seek the good as it is for water to run downhill – though perhaps there is something not quite appropriate in this comparison! It must also be asked whether Confucius was consistent in maintaining the natural goodness of humanity. If people have the drive toward goodness within them, then would not Lao-zu be right in simply letting them be? Confucius, on the other hand, wanted to change human society. He obviously thought there was something very far wrong with the Chinese society in which he had grown up. So at least the goodness of man could not be universal, but then we are driven toward the divisive idea that some are good and some are bad, that some are elect and some are reprobate, and the door seems to be opened to those very evils which Confucius wanted to overcome, namely, civil war and class war. Furthermore, one would have to ask why he found it necessary to lay so much stress on education, a topic to which we shall soon return.

How then does Confucius envisage the good man? It is unfortunate that in some English translations the 'good man' is designated by the term 'gentleman'. This, I say, is unfortunate because our term 'gentleman' is inescapably a class term, while Confucius is setting before us a moral ideal. Admittedly, even Confucius' ideal of the good man is not entirely free of what might be called 'bourgeois' connotations. The good man will be educated or cultivated – this again calls in question the notion of a natural goodness. But Confucius is clear that there is in every human being what might be called the 'raw material' of goodness, and that suitable education can bring this material to realization. If we understand him in this way, then his claim for a natural goodness in human beings begins to seem more plausible. Even someone who believed in original sin, as many

Christians have done, is bound to admit that nevertheless in the biblical creation story righteousness is more original than sin. Every human being has within himself or herself a mixture of good and evil, and presumably it is nurture or education, the influences received from other human beings, that constitute a major factor in enabling the good to preponderate in any individual life.

But the point that human beings do influence one another brings us to recognize something else, something of which Confucius was well aware. It is that no human being exists as an isolated entity. Every such being is a nexus of relationships tying his or her life inextricably into the lives of others. We have to understand what is motivating these others, and we do this by consulting our own motivations. This is perhaps as much a counsel of prudence as of morality, though of course prudence and morality are not simply to be set over against one another. The point is made in an exchange in which Confucius enunciates a negative form of the so-called 'Golden rule': a disciple asks him, 'is there a single word that can be a guide to conduct throughout one's life?' The Master replied, 'it is perhaps the word *shu* (that is to say, using oneself as a measure in gauging the wishes of others). Do not impose on others what you yourself do not desire'.[9] But if this in itself seems somewhat negative or at least minimalist, it is only the beginning of Confucius' sketch of the good man. But it is surely an indispensable foundation, the recognition that we share a common humanity, and that one's own desires and aspirations are located within an ocean of the desires and aspirations of others and that somehow these need to be regulated and harmonized among themselves. At least, we believe they should be harmonized if we are not content to accept that the state of nature is a state of war – and even if, like Hobbes, we did believe that, we would soon conclude with him that it is a nasty, brutish and generally intolerable state, and take steps to emerge from it. But can one get out of it only by the heavy exercise of despotic power acting in the interest of law and order, or have we, like Confucius and Locke, to go back and revise our idea of the state of nature and perhaps learn that it is people living together according to reason?

In working out the belief that there is a natural reciprocity in human relationships, Confucius goes back to the Chinese tradition and sees the family as the archetype of such relationships. Everyone knows that the Chinese have a veneration for their ancestors and that they respect the elderly. But while Confucius approves of such veneration and respect, he insists also on the reciprocity of these relationships. If the children of the family have an obligation to respect their parents, the father and mother have in turn an obligation to promote the well-being of their children. The political implications of this view are obvious. The subject of the state has an obligation to respect and obey the authority of the legitimate ruler, but the ruler has the obligation to seek the welfare of all his subjects and never to abuse his authority for the sake of self-interest.

Another affirmative aspect of the good person in Confucius' thinking is benevolence, a virtue which is constantly stressed. We may see this as an extension of the family ethic to all humanity, indeed, in one of his sayings he recognizes a brotherhood of all. The word usually translated 'benevolence' has the basic sense simply of 'humanity'. Perhaps the meaning and centrality of this conception can be best expressed through a catena of brief quotations: 'If a man sets his heart on benevolence, he will be free from evil. For men of benevolence, while it is inconceivable that they should seek to stay alive at the expense of benevolence, it may happen that they have to accept death in order to have benevolence accomplished. The good man never deserts benevolence, not even for as long as it takes to eat a meal; if he hurries and stumbles, one may be sure that it is in benevolence that he does so.'[10] But it is in connection with benevolence that we find a qualification of the doctrine of humanity's natural goodness. Confucius makes it clear that benevolence does not always come easily. He asks: 'Is there a man who for the space of a single day is able to devote all his strength to benevolence?'[11] But Confucius modestly said of himself, 'How dare I claim to be a sage or a benevolent man?'[12]

There are, of course, other virtues besides benevolence. In one saying. Confucius names a kind of triad of virtues – wisdom, benevolence and courage. Of wisdom, it is perhaps unnecessary to say anything, since Confucius' whole life was a pursuit of wisdom. Of course, it is clear that he was thinking more of moral courage than of physical courage: 'A benevolent man is sure to possess courage; a courageous man does not necessarily possess benevolence.'[13] Another important moral idea is that of rightness. If, for instance, a good man has an opportunity for gain, he will first think of what is right.

We have seen that Confucius became interested in moral and spiritual problems because of the appalling state of Chinese society in his time. In the foregoing sketch of 'the way' he commended, we have been thinking chiefly of individual human beings and their relations to one another. Confucius was aiming at the reordering of society, and this necessarily brought him into the political sphere. Probably the most revolutionary change that he was demanding was the move away from hereditary privilege to an entirely different system in which morality and intelligence would be the criteria. Where power is attained by birth into a royal or noble family, the person succeeding to such power is tempted to use it for personal advantage and to see himself as somehow the adversary of his subject people, rather than their leader in a co-operative venture aiming at the good of both ruler and people. This is how Confucius saw the significance of his moral principles for the state.

The application of Confucius' principles to the problems of government have been admirably summarized by H. G. Creel in six propositions, and I shall quote these:

> The proper aim of government is the welfare and happiness of the whole people.
>
> This aim can be achieved only when the state is administered by those most capable of government.
>
> Capacity to govern has no necessary connection with birth, wealth or position; it depends solely on character and knowledge.
>
> Character and knowledge are produced by proper education.
>
> In order that the best talents may become available, education should be widely diffused.
>
> It follows that the government should be administered by those persons, chosen from the whole population, who prove themselves to have profited most by the proper kind of education.[14]

Is this democracy? It is certainly a significant step toward democracy, though, as Creel points out, neither Confucius nor any other ancient Chinese thinker appears to have thought of voting, a practice already in use among the Greeks, and surely essential to a genuine democracy.

But Confucius does make a great stride toward democracy in his ideas about education. He did not embrace a foolish egalitarianism, but he did believe that education should be available to all who have the intelligence and the diligence to profit from it. Such people could be found in all sections of the population. He himself seems to have been willing to teach any who came to him and had teachable minds and willingness to apply themselves, regardless of social background. Thus one might say that the kind of democracy he envisaged was at the same time a meritocracy. Although it did not come until many centuries after Confucius, the public examination system for filling vacancies in the Chinese civil service was a result of his teachings.

So far I have made only the briefest mention of the religious aspect of Confucius' teaching, though in this regard I am merely following his own practice. It is, however, an important aspect and we must now pay attention to it. I have mentioned already that there is a type of religion which is not much concerned with the *minutiae* of theology but more with the significance of faith for human life in the world, and that is the type we find in Confucius. In such cases the practical or political teaching sometimes gets separated from the religion in which it originated, and continues as a purely secular doctrine. I suppose that could have happened in the particular case of Confucius. The social and political teaching could stand by itself, without a religious complement. It is true that in *The Analects* we are told that 'the topics the Master did not speak of were prodigies, forces and the gods'.[15] Also, he tended to brush off questions to which there are no certain answers. 'Chi-lu asked how the spirits of the dead and the gods should be served. The master said, "you are not able even to serve men. How can you serve the spirits?" Chi-lu persisted: "May I ask about death?" "You do not understand even life. How can you understand death?".'[16]

The principal religious idea in Confucius is Tien or Heaven. This was an idea already current, and is broadly equivalent to 'God', though it is apparently impersonal, while being at the same time moral. Perhaps the closest approximation in English would be the word 'Providence'. Tien seems to send to human beings a destiny or vocation for them to fulfil. Confucius believed that he had received his virtue from heaven, and by 'virtue' is meant not his moral virtues but rather the power to engage in his reforming mission. This is something different from what he obtained through education and study. It is rather the 'raw material' of a person's character, which is the endowment of heaven, but which needs to be shaped by education and by the person's own efforts. Elsewhere we read: 'Where there is a preponderance of native substance over acquired refinement, the result will be churlishness. When there is a preponderance of refinement over native substance, the result will be pedantry. Only a well-balanced admixture of these two will result in the good man.'[17] Might we suppose that there is an analogy between the virtue or power which Confucius believed had been conferred on him by Heaven and the 'native substance', including the desire for good, which he saw as the raw material of human beings, awaiting the 'refinement' of the proper education? If this is a legitimate inference, then Tien would seem to be the author of the moral law and of the implantation in the human heart of the love of that law and delight in it. We can say, I think, that Tien is not interventionist. So when Confucius was ill and one of the disciples asked permission to offer a prayer, the Master replied that he had long been offering prayers, presumably meaning that for a long time he had been obeying the vocation sent to him by Tien. On the other hand, he made remarks which seem to indicate that he believed that Tien's providential activity could be seen in large-scale events, such as the rise and fall of cultures.

It is not only intercessory prayer about which Confucius is negative or at best ambiguous. Surprisingly, meditation is rather sharply dismissed. 'I once spent all day meditating without taking food, and all night meditating without going to bed, but I gained nothing from it. It would have been better for me to have spent the time in learning.'[18] Sacrifices were common in China, but while Confucius was an advocate of respect for ancestors, he believed that most sacrifices were made in order to gain benefits for the sacrificer, and he had no use for such self-regarding actions. As we know, he believed that virtue is its own reward. What would he have thought if he had known that one day the Emperor would be offering sacrifices to Confucius! The barbarous custom of human sacrifice had been not uncommon in China before Confucius' time. Wives, concubines, slaves might be put to death with a ruler when he died. Confucius opposed this practice, and even the custom of burying with the ruler, human statues, as a substitute, like the army of terracotta soldiers discovered in recent times at Xian. But unfortunately Confucius' humanitarian efforts did not prevent, as we noted earlier, 460 of his own followers from being buried alive by order of the first Emperor at the time of the burning of the books.

One part of religion which Confucius highly valued was ceremonial or rites (*li*). This again may seem surprising in one who seemed to value religion mainly as a support for morality, because many who have thought in that way have been indifferent to the ceremonial side of religion or have even attacked it as a diversion from the ethical side. One thinks, for instance, of the Hebrew prophets who declared that God demands not sacrifices but right-eousness; or of Immanual Kant at the time of the Enlightenment, for his *Religion within the Limits of Reason Alone* has many affinities with Confucius' thought, both in keeping God in the background and in holding that the true worship of God consists in conscientious action; or of Matthew Arnold in the nineteenth century, who held that religion is, in the main, conduct, and whose idea of God as 'a Power not ourselves making for righteousness' has a remarkable resemblance to Confucius' understanding of Tien.

But the fact remains that Confucius was quite sticky about ceremonial. He claims, for instance, that in his time people approaching the altar made an obeisance only when they got to the top of the steps, whereas he continued to observe the old custom of making his obeisance at the bottom of the steps before going up. This alone shows a spirit of reverence, which is surely at the very core of religion. But Confucius' appreciation of ceremonial was based on something deeper. He did not see rites and moral action as in any way rival claimants for our attention. The ritual actions that we perform help to shape our characters. Perhaps subconsciously, they impress truths upon us. They mediate between belief and action. As Confucius saw it, they help to ensure that our conduct follows 'the way'. A good example is provided by the funeral rites, which were important both for Confucians and for the Chinese in general. These rites channelled the conduct of the mourners, allowing neither for an apathy in the presence of death nor for an excessive grief. We may remember at this point the story about the funeral of Lao-zu.[19] In this matter, Confucius could claim like Buddha that he follows a middle way.

Sadly, it is often the case that the teaching of a mediator who brings to his people a new vision of God and a new understanding of their own lives, deteriorates at the hands of his successors. Religion seems to be one of those areas of life where the beginning is the strongest, and as time goes on, there is just as likely to be decay as development. Not long after the persecution by the first Emperor, the fortunes of Confucianism changed, and in the third century CE it became the state religion of China. Historians have compared this event to the change in the fortunes of Christianity, when after three centuries of persecution under the Roman Empire, it became under Constantine first a licit religion and then eventually the religion of the Empire. Those events, whether in China or in the Mediterranean lands seemed like a great victory, perhaps the work of divine Providence. But in both cases, the results were equivocal. Peace with the state and the privileges that the state granted meant also that religion was now harnessed to the state. To be sure, some of Confucius' basic ideas survived and still survive today, but there has been a heavy price to pay.

All religions in China have been through a 'fiery trial' since the coming of the communist regime in 1949. But a religion that has existed for 2500 years and has so deeply moulded the Chinese character has surely a future in the inscrutable purpose of Heaven.

6

Socrates

(470–399 BCE)

Can we justify including Socrates among the mediators? Admittedly, there is no religion called after him, no such thing as 'Socratism', comparable, say, to Confucianism or Zoroastrianism. According to Cicero, Socrates called down philosophy from heaven to earth by abandoning cosmological and metaphysical inquiries in order to concentrate on ethics. Cicero approved of this change: 'I cannot but the more admire the wisdom of Socrates, who ... affirmed that these inquiries concerning the secrets of nature were either above the efforts of human reason or were absolutely of no consequence at all to human life.'[1] Socrates was like Confucius in making ethics his primary concern, but this does not rule out his significance for religion. His influence was great in that phase of Greek religion which Walter Burkert has called 'philosophical religion', and which he introduces by saying, 'With the rise of philosophy, the most significant achievement of the Greeks in shaping the intellectual tradition of mankind, change and revolution is finally seen to irrupt into the static structures of Greek religion.'[2] It is true that even in its philosophical forms Greek religion has become a thing of the past, but much of its spirit passed into Christianity to blend with its Hebrew heritage. Socrates has had an honoured place in the Christian tradition. In the very early days of the church, St Justin Martyr declared: 'Those who lived by the Word are Christians, even though they have been considered atheists, such as, among the Greeks, Socrates, Heraclitus and others like them.'[3] Socrates was in fact tried and condemned on a charge which included 'impiety' (*asebeia*), and we shall consider this charge later. But his religious beliefs were important for him, even if they are overshadowed by his ethical concerns. In any case, whatever he may have believed about God or the gods, no one could deny that he expounded and championed the spiritual nature of man, and that is surely a doctrine just as essential to religion as belief in God.

Ancient Greek religion, like that of India and many other countries, was polytheistic, and we are all familiar through our reading of Homer and other classical writers with the brilliant Greek pantheon, headed by Zeus, father of the gods and god of justice. But the vast corpus of myths that had grown up around the figures of the gods were little influenced by any moral conceptions, whether of justice or any other virtue. With the rise of philosophy, these ancient myths were criticized. Socrates himself is represented in Plato's *Republic* as a powerful critic of the stories of the gods as found in the poets, and he would have had them excluded from the education of the young. (Perhaps the views expressed in *The Republic* are those of Plato himself, but there can be little doubt that what is said about the gods of traditional religion would be also the view of Socrates.) But Socrates was not an atheist in the sense of one who denies the existence of any god. Some of the sophists had taken up an atheistic or agnostic stance, but Socrates did not follow them. On the other hand, it is very doubtful if one could think of Socrates as a monotheist – this question will be discussed later. He probably continued to pay outward respect to the gods of the pantheon, and may well have continued to believe that they exist. For instance, he would greet the rising sun with a kiss, he believed that Apollo had called him to a mission to the Greeks, and on his deathbed, he reminded his friend Crito that the sacrifice of a cock was due to Asclepius. According to Xenophon, 'He was frequently seen sacrificing at home and on the public altars of the city.'[4] He may, of course, have thought of these several gods as simply different manifestations of the one whom he sometimes called simply 'God', perhaps understood also as Zeus, the father of all. Or like some of the other mediators, he may have had some idea of a God beyond the gods. In any case, to whatever extent he distanced himself from the gods of the pantheon, this was due not to a rejection of the divine, but to a new emphasis on morality. A human being who had become aware of his or her spiritual nature could not offer worship to beings whose behaviour was immoral even by human standards. So although Socrates devoted his thinking mostly to ethics, this could not fail to affect what he believed about God. We can indeed recognize him as a mediator, and in fact he falls right in the middle of that epoch which Jaspers called the 'axial age'.[5]

Our next question must be, 'What are the sources for our knowledge of Socrates?' There are several sources, and our difficulty here is not the paucity of the information, but the difficulty of deciding which source to follow when they conflict. There are three main sources. (1) The Dialogues of Plato. Three of these, the *Apology*, *Crito*, and *Phaedo* are regarded by many critics as a kind of memorial tribute by Plato to his old teacher. Socrates appears in other dialogues of Plato, but sometimes he is simply the mouthpiece for Plato's own philosophy. In the latest dialogues, Socrates disappears from the scene. In some dialogues from Plato's middle period, it is hard to know whether Socrates' contribution represents his own thinking or Plato's – we have already seen an example of this, namely, the teaching in the *Republic* that myths and fables about the gods should be removed from the school curriculum. Attempts have, of course, been made to isolate the 'genuine' Socratic teaching, but there are many opinions about this. (2) Some writings of Xenophon, especially the *Memorabilia*, *Symposium* and *Apology*. This evidence does not conflict in any fundamental way with Plato's picture, but one might say that Xenophon interprets Socrates in a more 'worldly' way, Plato in a more spiritual. (3) Some of the comedies of Aristophanes, especially *The Clouds* introduce Socrates as one of the characters. Greek comedy was even coarser and more libellous than what passes for comedy in the twentieth century. Socrates is represented as pursuing absurd researches into matters remote from public interest in what is contemptuously called a 'thoughtshop'. Aristophanes is writing burlesque, so that his picture cannot be taken as seriously contradicting the more sober ones of Plato and Xenophon. But A. E. Taylor makes the point that whereas Plato's three definitely Socratic dialogues are showing us Socrates at seventy years of age, Aristophanes shows us Socrates twenty-five years earlier in his life, so perhaps he was different then – there is reason to believe that before he turned to human ethical problems, he had been interested in more remote questions.[6]

Critics have probably exaggerated the differences among the sources and have not left enough room for development and change in Socrates himself. There has been a search for the 'historical Socrates' as an abstraction to be distilled from the various sources. Perhaps Taylor was thinking of the parallel search for the somewhat uninteresting 'historical Jesus' when he wrote: 'The "historical Socrates", of whom nineteenth-century writers had much to say, meant, in fact, the Socrates of Plato, with the genius taken out of him.'[7] But in the case of Socrates, one is at least spared the problem of myth, so troublesome in the case of some of the other mediators. Socrates remains from beginning to end a thoroughly human and credible character, though certainly an extraordinary one.

The birth of Socrates can be dated to 470 BCE. His parents appear to have been quite well off and Socrates received a good education. Also he does not seem to have needed to earn a living, and so was able to devote his time to the pursuit of knowledge.[8] At first his interest was directed toward the natural sciences. But Socrates' interests were not narrowly academic. There was another side to him which we might vaguely call 'mystical'. According to Plato, Socrates explained this aspect of his experiences as follows: 'You have heard me speak at many times and places of a divine sign from God which comes to me . . . This sign, which is a kind of voice, first began to come to me when I was a child; it is negative, forbidding me to do things but never positively commanding me to do anything.'[9] This is about as fully as Socrates ever describes the sign. It is sometimes called his *daimon*, understood as a divine inner voice. Could it be compared to the 'inner light' which some Quakers have claimed to have experienced, or to revelatory experiences, like those of Moses and Zoroaster? The comparison is certainly not an exact one, for we have seen that Socrates stressed the negative character of the voice. It warned him against taking some action, but did not give him affirmative guidance. Whatever the nature of this divine sign may have been or whatever its explanation, it did play an important part in Socrates' life. He also had moments of rapture or trance, one of which lasted a whole day.

Quite early in Socrates' career, there took place an event which was, for him, virtually a revelation, and one that determined the remainder of his story. A friend of his, Chaerophon by name, visited the Delphic oracle, and inquired of the god (Apollo) whether anyone was wiser than Socrates. The answer was that no one was wiser than he, and this answer was duly communicated to Socrates himself. At first he could not believe it, for he was deeply conscious of his own ignorance. But surely the god would not lie. Socrates determined to test the answer, and the method he devised was this: he would go to persons who had a reputation for wisdom and question them. If he found that one or more of them were really wise, then he would have refuted the oracle. So he began examining likely candidates – first politicians, then poets and finally artisans. But in each case the pretended wisdom of these men broke down under questioning. Socrates was better off than any of them, because they in fact knew nothing, though they thought that they knew quite a lot. Socrates had the advantage of them, for although he knew no more than they did, he at least did not entertain the erroneous belief that he possessed knowledge.[10]

He believed then that God (Apollo) had called him to a mission, namely, to awaken his fellow citizens to their true state of ignorance. Only when they had recognized that this was indeed their real condition would they be able seriously to pursue wisdom. So from then on Socrates spent his time in discussion with individuals or small groups, but the topics discussed were problems of ethics and politics, rather than problems of natural science. He gathered around him a group of associates, such as Alcibiades, a brilliant but irresponsible young man, Critias, a man of great wealth, and then later on Crito and Plato, who were to stand by him in his troubles. Already in his forties, Socrates was a well-known figure in Athens, as is proved by the fact that he was made the target of Aristophanes' ridicule.

It would be a mistake to think that Socrates' philosophical activity was merely negative and destructive. Certainly, mistaken ideas had to be got out of the way before anything constructive could be done, but in the process new and important ideas began to emerge.

Perhaps the one for which Socrates is chiefly remembered is his doctrine of the soul (*psyche*). The soul, he believed, is the centre and the most valuable element in a human being. Before Socrates' time, soul meant simply 'life', but with him it took on a meaning which might be expressed by the word 'personhood', a conscious reality capable of thinking and knowing, of choosing and acting. Various influences may have encouraged Socrates to think about the soul as he did. The Orphic mysteries may have had something to do with it.[11] Again, the philosopher Anaxagoras had come to Athens about the time of Socrates' birth, and lived there for thirty years. Socrates got to know of his teaching that mind (*nous*) is the cause of everything, though he says he was disappointed when he studied Anaxagoras' views in detail. At any rate, Socrates' teaching was that the Athenians should be less concerned with money and prestige, and more concerned with cultivating the soul. It was to this end that he examined them and tried to awaken them from complacency, acting,

as he expressed it himself, like a kind of gadfly on the body politic of
Athens. He was teaching the citizens that, in his own famous phrase,
'the unexamined life is not worth living'.[12] Doubtless they should
have been grateful for his teaching, but in fact they resented it, just as
later the Pharisees were to resent Jesus' exposure of the shallowness
of their faith.

The other major contribution of Socrates was his doctrine of
forms, though here we are on less sure ground, since it cannot be said
with certainty how much this doctrine owes to Socrates and how
much to Plato. Still, there can be little doubt that the origins go back
to Socrates. It is part of his quest for wisdom. Knowledge, as distinct
from mere opinion, possesses certainty and permanence. These are
never fully attainable when our attention has the sensible world as its
object. Only with forms is knowledge, in the strictest sense,
attainable. The geometer, for instance, discovers the properties of
the triangle, but not the triangle that we draw on paper. The
geometer is concerned with the ideal triangle, an intelligible object
perceived by the mind, not the senses. The objects perceived by the
senses participate, but never fully, in the ideal forms. Sensible forms
come into being and pass out of being, but the forms remain
unchanged. Supreme among these forms is the form of the Good.
The form of the Good is a kind of providence (*pronoia*), ensuring
that all things are ordered as best they may be. In some respects, the
form of the Good has the characteristics of God, yet it seems to be
impersonal. Perhaps it could be compared with Tien (Heaven) in
Confucius' thought. In the *Republic*, Socrates compares the place of
the form of the Good in the intelligible world to that of the sun in the
world of sense. (Here again, we must bear in mind the *caveat* that it is
uncertain where the beliefs of Socrates merge into those of Plato.)
The highest knowledge that we could attain is knowledge of the form
of the Good. And this would also be virtue (*arete*), the bringing of the
human being to the highest level possible for that being.

I have mentioned earlier the possibility that for Socrates, as for
some of the other mediators we have considered, there may be a 'God
beyond the gods'. Is this the form of the Good, the source not only of
the visible world but even of Zeus and the other gods? It is possible
that something of the sort is implied in some words of Socrates at his
trial, when he is replying to the charge that he is an atheist. He says: 'I
do believe that there are gods, and in a sense higher than that in
which any of my accusers believe in them.' It seems reasonable to

suppose that this 'higher sense' refers to a belief in the form of the Good as highest reality.[13]

Before we come to the last phase in Socrates' career, it may be as well to sketch in the historical background in which his life was set. About a decade before his birth, the victory of the Greek forces at the battle of Plataea had finally turned back the Persian army which for a long time had been threatening to subjugate Greece. Then there opened for Athens a period of prosperity and expansion, in which it became the centre of a great trading empire in the eastern Mediterranean. But this period was not of long duration. In 431 BCE there began the Peloponnesian War. Apart from a short break, this was continued until 404. The enemies of Athens had combined under the leadership of Sparta to challenge its supremacy, and they were at last successful. When a country is smarting under defeat in war, the usual tendency is to look for a scapegoat. This was the moment when the Athenians turned on Socrates, and in 399 he was brought to trial. R. W. Livingstone quotes the actual words of the indictment as follows: 'Meletus, son of Meletus, a member of the tribe of Pitthus, against Socrates, son of Sophroniscus, of the tribe of Alopeke. Socrates is guilty of not believing in the gods in whom the state believes, and of introducing other strange divinities; and he is also guilty of corrupting the young. Penalty death.'

How was it possible that such charges could be brought against a philosopher who believed that he was working—indeed, had a divine mission to work – for the good of Athens; a philosopher, furthermore, who was, as we have seen, a believer in God, if not in the gods, and who had a lively sense that he was guided by a supernatural sign; and finally a philosopher who had taught, apparently without payment, many young men who were searching for knowledge?

It was possible, and it actually happened. Nor can one say that those who accused Socrates were acting only out of malice. From their point of view, however biased it may have been, they did believe that they had a case. More than that, they persuaded the 'jury', consisting for the most part, we may suppose, of decent Athenian citizens, that Socrates was guilty. It should be added that the jury consisted of between five hundred and six hundred citizens who were both judge and jury, according to the procedures of Athenian law.

In his response to the accusations, Socrates begins by defending himself against the charge of atheism. He thinks that the origin of the charge may go back to the comedy of Aristophanes, which had been presented about a quarter of a century before the trial. In that play, he had been represented as a sophist, understood as one who dabbles in abstruse questions and who uses rhetoric to 'make the worse appear the better cause'. Some of the sophists were in fact atheists, notably Protagoras, author of the well-known saying that 'man is the measure of all things'. But Socrates seeks to dissociate himself from these sophists, both from some of their teachings and from their alleged greed for fees from their students. He has never run a school or had an organized body of students, but has simply discussed with any people who were willing to converse with him. 'Reflecting that I was really too honest a man to be a politician, I did not go where I could do no good to you or to myself; but where I could do the greatest good privately to every one of you, thither I went, and sought to persuade every man among you that he must look to himself and seek virtue and wisdom, before he looks to his private interests, and care more for Athens than he cares for the affairs of Athens.'[14]

If the accusations of impiety seemed plausible to the jurors, perhaps it was a case of guilt by association. Some of Socrates' associates were far from measuring up to his own standards. We have seen that Aristophanes had associated him with the sophists, had indeed made him into a sophist. Then there was his friendship with Alcibiades, who was alleged to have burlesqued the Eleusinian mysteries. We have seen too how Socrates was drawn and then repelled by the thought of Anaxagoras. The books of this philosopher had been burned in Athens, and the philosopher himself exiled from the city on the ground of impiety. The heavenly bodies were in those days still considered to be divine beings. Anaxagoras had been rash enough to teach that the sun is a mass of white-hot metal, bigger than the Peloponnese.

As regards the charge that he had corrupted the youth, once again guilt by association told against Socrates. He and Alcibiades had been close friends. When the two of them were on military service together at the beginning of the Peloponnesian War, Socrates had saved the younger man's life at considerable risk to his own. But Alcibiades had become thoroughly unpopular in Athens. We have already noted his mockery of the Eleusinian mysteries. He had also let down Athens very badly during the war. In 415 he had advocated an expedition against Syracuse, and this ended in disaster. Later he had actually gone over to the Spartan side. He was already dead by the time Socrates was put on trial, but he had left a bad memory behind him, and Socrates was blamed for having led him astray. In fact, there is not the slightest reason for supposing that Socrates had been anything other than a good influence with a very wayward and spoiled young man, but in the bitterness of defeat after the war, Athenians could be stirred to suspicion without any substantial evidence.

When Socrates had made his defence against the indictment, the jury voted on the question of his guilt or innocence. By a majority of sixty they found him guilty. This was quite a narrow majority, considering the large number of jurors. As Socrates himself observed, if only thirty out of the 500 or so had voted the other way, he would have been acquitted.

Now we come to another peculiarity of Athenian law. We have seen that the prosecutors had asked for the death penalty. It was the custom in Athens to permit the accused, if found guilty, to propose an alternative penalty to the one demanded, and then there might be a bit of bargaining. Historians are broadly agreed that if, for instance, Socrates had proposed exile instead of death, this would have been accepted. It is suggested that the prosecutors expected this – perhaps they knew that making martyrs eventually rebounds upon those who do such a thing. But Socrates was uncompromising, and may have felt that any move on his side would be interpreted as weakness, or even an admission of guilt. So in words that anticipated the Christian apostles of a later age, he declared: 'Men of Athens, I have the warmest affection for you; but I shall obey God rather than you, and while I have life and strength, I shall never cease from the practice and teaching of philosophy, exhorting anyone whom I meet and saying to him after my manner, "You, my friend, a citizen of the great and mighty and wise city of Athens, are you not ashamed of devoting yourself to acquiring the greatest amount of money and honour and reputation, and caring so little about wisdom and truth and the greatest improvement of the soul, which you never regard or heed at all?"'[15] He maintained that if he got what he deserved, it would not be a lesser punishment, but rather, a public honour, perhaps a free apartment in the Guildhall! This, of course, was Socratic irony, and it was not well received. So he offered to pay a nominal fine of one mina, a large silver coin worth about $20. Some of his friends in court, including Plato and Crito, persuaded him to raise the amount to 30 mina. They offered to guarantee this amount, for Socrates now claimed that he was quite poor. This was not due to any high living, for he had always lived very simply and dressed quite plainly. The change in his financial situation was probably due to losses occasioned by the war.

In any case, the jurors felt that Socrates had treated the possibility of receiving a reduced punishment in a derisory manner, and they now voted by a larger majority than on the first occasion to carry out the death sentence.

In the Athens of that time, the death sentence was effected by giving to the condemned a drink of poison – in Socrates' case, it was a draught of hemlock. Normally this lethal drink was given within twenty-four hours of the passing of sentence, but in Socrates' case it was delayed for a special reason. Each year Athens sent a sacred ship to Delos to take part in the festival of Apollo. Until that ship returned, executions were delayed. The ship had left shortly before the beginning of Socrates' trial.

So we now pass from the *Apology*, the first scene in Plato's account of the last days of Socrates, to the *Crito*, the second scene. Socrates is in prison and it is early morning, with dawn just breaking. A month has passed from the trial. Socrates is still sleeping, when the door is opened and his friend Crito enters. Crito has come to tell him that the ship has now reached Cape Sunium and should arrive at Athens (or rather at Piraeus, the port of Athens), later in the day. So he tells Socrates that 'tomorrow will be the last day of your life'. But he gets a curious answer which throws further light on the 'mystical' side of Socrates. 'Very well, Crito,' he says, 'if such is the will of God, I am willing; but my belief is that there will be the delay of a day', and he goes on to say that he has had a vision during the night in which a shining figure brought him a coded message which he understood to mean that his life would be spared until the day after next.

The *Crito* is perhaps the most dramatic of Plato's three dialogues written about the end of Socrates. Crito announces to Socrates that the way of escape is open to him. He has, presumably, bribed the keeper of the prison – he has 'done him a favour', as he puts it. I suppose no one would have blamed Socrates if he had taken the opportunity to escape. He believed himself that he had been unjustly condemned. Within a few hours he could have been out of the small city-state of Athens and into territory where the Athenian laws could not reach him. Surely it was enough that he had had the courage to face the trial, without also having to face death?

But Socrates is determined to turn down the temptation to escape. Why did he turn it down? The reason he gave was that, even if the sentence was unjust, he had been tried according to the laws of Athens and he owed obedience to the state. More important than saving one's life is the duty to live a blameless life. If he fled to some neighbouring city-state, he would indeed live, but he would be living with the consciousness of being a law-breaker. I must confess that I am not entirely satisfied with this explanation. It seems to be inconsistent with what Socrates had said during the trial. There we heard the bold words, 'I shall obey God rather than you!' There is a law of God or of the Good which, as pure ideal form, ranks above all historical and therefore imperfect laws, such as the law of Athens. But now Socrates seems to be ascribing an absolute authority to the law of the state.

If then the explanation which Plato has put into Socrates' mouth is not the correct one, what is? Surely not that Socrates was courting martyrdom in the belief that by so doing he would best serve the cause of truth and justice? Undoubtedly it has been the martyrdom of Socrates that has profoundly impressed generations of men and women and has served the cause which he treasured. But while he accepted that martyrdom, I do not think he courted it as a device to sway opinion. In his trial, he had made it clear he would rely on rational argument, not on any emotional appeal.

I think myself that what was really decisive for Socrates was the fact that Crito and his other friends would have to use bribery in order to deliver him from execution. In other words, they would have to corrupt the souls of those who could prevent Socrates' escape, and their own souls would be corrupted in the process. A former Glasgow professor of moral philosophy, A. A. Bowman, was a prisoner-of-war in the Great War of 1914–18. Reflecting on his experiences, he would say that morally it was perfectly legitimate to seek escape, even by the use of violence. But what would be morally wrong would be to bribe the guards, for that would demand the corruption of a human being. Bowman was deeply immersed in Platonism, and though I do not believe he ever mentioned Socrates in connection with his own experience of imprisonment, the comparison might well have been there in his mind. In any case, I am suggesting that the inevitable corruption of human beings in Crito's plan for escape may well have been the most powerful reason for Socrates' rejection of the plan.

We pass on to the *Phaedo*, by far the longest of the three dialogues
we are considering. It gives a detailed account of Socrates' last day
alive, which he spent in discussion with his friends in the prison.
Much of it is taken up with arguments concerning the immortality of
the soul. It elaborates and carries further those teachings about the
soul and about the forms as the true objects of knowledge which we
outlined above as Socrates' basic philosophy.[16] But here the question
again has to be raised about how much of this teaching comes from
Socrates himself, and how much is due to Plato. That is a question
which need not be treated in the context of this book. We have
learned enough about Socrates to appreciate his significance as a
mediator, and what we have learned is securely based, so that we are
not dependent on the very risky business of trying to decide whether
this or that argument in the *Phaedo* is originally derived from
Socrates himself. These arguments for the immortality of the soul
would in any case carry little weight in modern discussion. The
greatness and significance of Socrates can stand without them.

In this connection, it may be worthwhile to mention that only a
month before his death, in the remarks he made after the jury had
confirmed the death-sentence, Socrates did not declare an unequiv-
ocal belief in a life beyond death, but contemplated with equanimity
two possibilities, a life beyond the grave or simply extinction. He
claimed that either of these would be a gain. Let me quote his words:

> There is great reason to hope that death is a good. There are two
> alternatives; death is a state of nothingness and utter unconscious-
> ness, or, as men say, there is a migration of the soul from this world
> to another. Now if you suppose that there is no consciousness, but
> a sleep like the sleep of him who is undisturbed even by dreams,
> death will be an unspeakable gain. Now, if death be of such a
> nature, I say that to die is gain; for eternity is then only a single
> night. But if death is the journey to another place, and there, as
> men say, all the dead abide, what good can be greater than this?[17]

The second alternative is better than the first, but both are gains. Is it
likely that Socrates' beliefs on the question would have changed so
greatly in the course of a month? It is possible, for we are told that to
be awaiting death brings about a wonderful concentration of the
mind. But it seems to me more likely that for Socrates the hope of
immortality remained a hope, and that he would have been almost
equally accepting of the alternative. It is perhaps significant that

Xenophon's account of Socrates' defence makes no mention of life beyond death. It is perhaps enough to recall the final words of Plato's *Apology*: 'The hour of departure has come, and we go our ways, I to die and you to live. Which is better is known only to God.'[18]

As was said at the beginning of this chapter, there is no religion of Socratism. But he still has a message for all religions. It lies in the close connection which he saw between virtue and knowledge. He may have gone too far in seemingly identifying the two, and perhaps underestimating the moral struggle when someone knows the good but weakness prevents its realization. But he was right in making knowledge and virtue, truth and goodness, inseparable. The message for the religions is that they cannot survive without both moral and intellectual integrity, not the one without the other.

Krishna

(Third Century BCE)

Among the 'mediators' whom we are considering in this book, Krishna is one of the most elusive, as far as historical information about him is concerned. Just as Christian scholars have engaged in the so-called 'quest for the historical Jesus', so students of Hinduism have pursued a quest for the historical Krishna. I have no doubt myself that there was a historical Krishna, and if I thought otherwise, then obviously I would not have included him among the mediators who brought about important new understandings of God among their fellow human beings. Even if such persons came eventually to be considered in some cases as themselves divine beings, they could have fulfilled their mission only if they had been members of the human race, speaking a human language and living in the human condition.

There has, in fact, been a continuous tradition for about two thousand years that Krishna was born in the city of Mathura, situated between Delhi and Agra. If you visit that city today, you will find in it a house, outside which is a notice: BIRTHPLACE OF KRISHNA! I do not say it is authentic, any more than I would vouch for the authenticity of the Grotto of the Nativity in Bethlehem. But that entire area round Mathura is soaked in traditions relating to Krishna, and this is most easily explained by supposing that he did in fact once live there, though the facts of his life are now concealed in a dense mass of legend.[1]

The main tradition about Krishna is contained in the great Indian epic poem, *Mahabharata*.[2] According to the poem, Krishna was the son of a provincial prince, Vasudeva, who came to be regarded as a kind of demigod, and whose name was sometimes used for Krishna himself. So we learn from the historian Masson-Oursel that 'in Udaipur, an inscription of about 150 BC mentions Vasudeva, another name of Krishna'. The same historian mentions also a line from the same period, which runs, 'May the power of Krishna increase!'³ Krishna's uncle was a certain Kamsa, king of Mathura, and he turns out to be the Herod of this story. He was brother to Krishna's mother, Devaki, and Kamsa had been told of a prophecy that one of Devaki's children would kill him, so he gave orders that all her children should be killed. Vasudeva and Devaki were able to transport Krishna out of Mathura to a cowherding community on the other side of the River Jumna, and there Krishna grew up under the tutelage of the headman of the community and his wife.

As happened with other religious leaders, stories were told of miracles done by the youthful Krishna. These were quite fanciful, though there may be symbolic truth behind the story of his quarrel with the ancient Vedic god Indra, for this was the time when India was turning away from the old deities to new ones, of whom Krishna was destined to become one of the most popular. But alongside the stories of miracles were other stories which represent him as a mischievous child and later as an amorous youth whose sweet playing on the flute drew the maidens of the community into the forest where they danced and sported with Krishna. One of these girls, Radha, became his consort. In due time, Krishna returned to Mathura, fulfilled the prophecy by killing Kamsa, and ruled in his stead.

That might have been the end of the story, and perhaps it was the end of that cycle of Krishna legends which are placed in the rural community. But according to the *Mahabharata*, Krishna left Mathura after a few years and became involved in a famous war between two rival but related dynasties, the Kurus and the Pandavas. There may have been such a war at an early period of Indian history, just as there may have been (and presumably was) a Trojan War in the early days of Greece, but both of these have been so mythologized that we have virtually no historical information about them. But it was in the course of this war that Krishna gave the religious and moral teaching that has become inseparably associated with his name. We shall consider this teaching further on in our study, but meanwhile I shall finish this sketch of his career, still following the *Mahabharata*. The Pandavas were eventually victorious, but soon after the end of hostilities, Krishna died. The story is reminiscent of the story of the death of Achilles in Greek legend. Because he was an incarnation or *avatar* of the high god Vishnu, Krishna was for the most part invulnerable, and in the various legends in the earlier parts of the epic, he had turned aside sword thrusts and other hazards without sustaining any injury. But at one point a sage, in a moment of anger, had cursed him and prophesied that he would die from a wound in the foot. Krishna was sitting quietly meditating in the forest when a huntsman saw him and, mistaking him for a deer, discharged an arrow. It pierced Krishna in the left heel and wounded him fatally. The hunter was overcome with distress at what he had done, but with his last breath Krishna comforted him and told him not to fear. Though the story looks like another legend, it does tell us something of importance, namely, that Krishna was truly a human being and believed to be such. Gods do not die, but all human beings die.

What do we make of this story of Krishna? Many scholars believe that, while there may well have been a historical Krishna, the figure represented in the tradition is a composite figure, and it may be that the person whom we call 'Krishna' is in fact two or more persons who have been merged together. There is a further complication when we remember that 'Krishna' is also the incarnation of Vishnu. An interesting fact about the name Krishna is that it connects with the root of the Sanskrit word for 'black'. Furthermore, in Indian art, Krishna has usually been represented with black or bluish-black features. I have never heard a satisfactory explanation of the bluish element, but the blackness has been plausibly explained on the hypothesis that Krishna was originally the name given to a deity of the early Dravidian-speaking inhabitants of India, and that this black god was incorporated into the Indian pantheon at the time when the old Vedic gods – see the reference to Indra above – were on the wane.

Can we suggest a possible date for this elusive mediator, Krishna? I have boldly put 'third century BCE' at the beginning of the chapter. There are some considerations that support this, though of course it could be wrong. We noted Masson-Oursel's mention of 150 BCE as a date when the Krishna cult appeared to be on the rise. We notice also the view of R. C. Zaehner that the material concerning Krishna in the *Mahabharata* is later than the Upanishads and later than the rise of Buddhism, since both seem to be presupposed pretty clearly in the *Bhagavadgita*,[4] to which we shall be turning very shortly. These evidences would seem to point to a time between about 400 and 100 BCE for the rise of the Krishna myth. We have to allow some time from the actual historical existence of Krishna (though in the India of that period, it could be a fairly short time!) to the point of development where he is exalted from the rank of hero to that of high god. So although the question is speculative, we may hope that we are not too far wrong. One result of this speculation, however, is that we have to acknowledge that the setting of the discourses of the *Bhagavadgita* in the context of the war between the Kurus and the Pandavas is quite fictitious. That war, if indeed it ever took place, was fought in the prehistorical period of India, long before the date we have assigned to Krishna. Admittedly, that date (third century BCE) was one that allowed wide margins of error, but hardly so wide that Krishna could be dated about a thousand years earlier, for the war in question is supposed to have taken place between 1400 and 1000 BCE, or possibly as late as 800 BCE. So how is the Krishna who lived among the cowherds, performed spectacular miracles, and eventually put paid to King Kamsa, related to the Krishna who, in the *Bhagavadgita* gives counsel to Arjuna? Of course, it might be replied that the date we have assigned to Krishna is simply wrong and that the 'historical Krishna' (or better: the 'prehistorical Krishna') must have lived far earlier than we have been led to suppose. But even if the evidence cited above for assigning to Krishna a date only two or three centuries before the beginning of the Christian era was fairly weak, there is the further evidence to which allusion was made, namely, the relatively late date of the *Bhagavadgita* itself. We recall Zaehner's point that the *Gita* contains ideas and even verbal echoes which derive from the *Upanishads* and from Buddhist writings, indicating a date later than 400 BCE. Some of this evidence is strong. When we read in the *Bhagavadgita*,

> Exalted are the senses (*indriyani*), or so they say; higher than the senses is the mind (*manas*); yet higher than the mind is the soul (*buddhi*); what is beyond the soul is He (i.e. the *Atman* or Universal Self).

This is virtually a quotation from the *Katha Upanishad*:

> Beyond the senses are the objects [of the senses], and beyond the objects is the mind; beyond the mind is the understanding (*buddhi*) and beyond the understanding is the Great Self (*Atman*).[5]

Likewise there are signs that the writer is familiar with Buddhism. Zaehner points to the use of a technical Buddhist term, and comments that the first chapters of the *Gita* are deeply influenced by Buddhism.[6]

So the association of Krishna with the ancient hero Arjuna is a literary device, and does not mean that we have to move Krishna back into a much earlier and virtually unknown period of time. But then the question arises more insistently: What is the relation between the Krishna of the rural community celebrated in the earlier parts of *Mahabharata* and the Krishna who discourses on profound moral and religious questions in the *Bhagavadgita*? The two may not be so far apart as they appear at first sight, and the editor or editors of the *Mahabharata* may not have been altogether wrong in presenting Krishna in two contrasting guises. On the one hand, he is a member of a rural community, often depicted engaged in agricultural labour, leading the oxen yoked to his plough with a mattock over his shoulder, or, when the day's labours are finished, playing his flute and participating in country merrymaking. This is the Krishna that has endeared himself to millions of ordinary Indians, a human figure who in this aspect is one of themselves. On the other hand is Krishna the sage and philosopher, versed in the subtle traditions of Indian thought, arguing about the nature of God and the nature of man, upholding the values of the personal after a long period in which the impersonal had been deemed of chief importance. This second Krishna has fascinated the wise men and leaders of India, from philosopher-theologians of the past, such as Shankara and Ramanuja, to such modern figures as Gandhi, and indeed the various Krishna movements have now gained a foothold in the Western world, and have thereby broken through the ethnic bounds of Hinduism.

What holds these two figures together is the substance of a common faith that is presented in two forms but which is basically a gospel of love. In the Krishna of the countryside, the message is presented in a popular form through stories and legends that are susceptible to allegorical interpretation and made to convey spiritual truths to people who have no aptitude for philosophical analysis and argumentation. The music of Krishna's flute which draws those who hear it into the forest is like the secret attraction of God drawing human beings into relation to himself. Even Krishna's amours, much elaborated in the popular writings known as *Puranas* can be (and are) interpreted as analogues of the love between God and his human creatures, a love interpreted in personal terms. The early Christian theologians followed the same path when they allegorized erotic parts of the Bible, such as *The Song of Songs*, and in this they themselves have been followed by many mystics.

The second Krishna, the Krishna of the *Gita*, brings the same essential message, but he does so in a much more sophisticated and conceptual way, and also in much greater detail. The *Gita* itself, of course, forms a part of the *Mahabharata*, though scholars disagree as to whether it originally belonged to the longer poem. However, as I have already said, I do not think that the editors were wrong in bringing together the two pictures. One might even say that it is not altogether impossible that the two Krishnas were originally one person who is being presented to us at different stages of his development. However, it is more likely that the second Krishna is the work of some erudite Indian scholar who had been so impressed by the essential truths underlying the legends about Krishna that he determined to give them a philosophical expression that would cause these truths to be taken seriously by the intellectual and spiritual leaders of his time, men steeped like himself in the traditional ideas and theories of Indian learning. Krishnaism, if we may use the term, was indeed a new departure in the history of Indian religion, but in our study of what we are calling 'mediators', we shall often be finding that religious innovations and new beginnings are not usually creations out of nothing but developments from traditions that have been exercising their influences for a very long time.

In the *Mahabharata* (including the *Bhagavadgita*) the two depictions of Krishna are linked together not only by being narrated as successive phases in the life of an individual, but are both regarded as *avatars* or descents of a high god, Vishnu, into the being of a human person, Krishna. Thus the two Krishnas (if one may so speak) are united by the indwelling of the divine Vishnu. In the stories of Krishna's early life in the cowherding community, it is told that one day the child's foster-mother had occasion to remove some mud from his mouth. Looking into his mouth, she saw within him the whole cosmos, and realized that this child was none other than a high god and contained within himself the entire world. In the mythological part of the epic, in which this particular incident is narrated, the presence of the divine power in Krishna is attested by signs and wonders, such as manifestations of superhuman strength. In the very different context of the *Bhadavadgita*, there is a parallel story of Krishna's revelation of his divine nature to Arjuna. This will call for fuller discussion later, but it may be said here that the revelation of Krishna's divinity in the *Gita* is primarily not through wonderful signs but through the wisdom of his teaching, if indeed that teaching is a sophisticated and conceptualized version of the spiritual truths implicit in the earlier legendary or quasi-mythological parts of the *Mahabharata*.

Should one speak of 'incarnation' in connection with the doctrine that Krishna is an *avatar* of Vishnu? In the introductory chapter of this book, I mentioned the case of an Indian student of mine who declared, 'In India, Christology is possible only as Krishnology',[7] and certainly there does seem to be a point of contact here between Christian and Krishnaist faith. Whether it is appropriate to use the word 'incarnation' in relation to both of these faiths obviously depends on just how one defines 'incarnation'. It is a difficult term. Christian theologians have been discussing the meaning of the incarnation in Jesus Christ for centuries and are still discussing it. Perhaps they have tried to be too precise, as, for instance, in the famous Chalcedonian formula of two 'natures' concurring in one 'person' or 'subsistence'. Indian thought does not lack a subtle vocabulary for describing the human person, but Indian theologians have, at least in the matter of the *avatars*, refrained from the speculative constructions that have been typical of Christian thought concerning incarnation. One obvious difference between the two faiths is that for Christianity there has been only one incarnation of the divine Logos, whereas in Hinduism certain gods have had several *avatars* or descents at different times. Vishnu, for example, is said to have had ten *avatars*, of which Krishna was the eighth.

But perhaps we should see the essence of both incarnation and *avatar* in the claim that the divine person 'comes down' or 'descends'. If this means self-humiliation or self-limitation on the part of deity, then it is indeed a revolutionary idea in the history of religion, and an idea that has a central place in both Christian and Krishnaist belief.

We have to go further still in asking about this common ground in the matter of the descent of the divine person. 'He came down from heaven', in the words of the Nicene Creed – a mythological expression, but one which can be readily interpreted in non-mythological terms. We can ask, 'Why did he come down?' Most Christian theologians from the New Testament onward have held that the descent or incarnation was for the salvation of the human race.[8] The *Bhagavadgita* gives a strikingly similar answer:

> Whensoever the law fails and lawlessness arises,
> I bring myself to embodied birth. To guard the righteous,
> I come to birth age after age.[9]

Admittedly, there are differences here. One of them we have noted already. Christian belief envisages a once-for-all incarnation and atonement. The Indian belief in *avatars* allows for a series of descents during the course of history, as human beings rise and then fall. I do not think that this is an irreconcilable difference. Sometimes a more serious difference has been alleged. It has been said that whereas Christian theologians have always insisted on the true and full humanity of Jesus Christ, Krishna is a docetic figure, a god in disguise who only seems to be human. This allegation is denied by A. C. Bouquet, who points out that Gandhi was considered by some Indians to be an *avatar*, but no one ever doubted that he was a human being, deeply immersed in human affairs![10] In any case, in spite of the credal statements of the church, many Christians have been docetic in their beliefs, perhaps unconsciously. It may be, however, that if anyone wants to talk about something so difficult as the question of how God can be so intimately related to a human being that incarnational language is appropriate, such language will inevitably be obscure and perhaps inconsistent according to strict logic.

We may push this problem of incarnational language even further. Its most important implication seems to be that the ultimate reality is a God who cares for his creatures, a God of love. According to the Krishna story, when the human creation sinks into lawlessness and decline, Vishnu 'comes down' from heaven to restore what is being destroyed. According to the Christian story, 'God so loved the world that he gave his only-begotten Son'. Probably neither story, however conceptualized we may try to make it, can finally escape some aura of the mythological. But in both cases we are hearing something of profound importance for the human race – what I called above a 'gospel of love', the good news that we can trust reality, that we can have faith in Being, that there is a God of love.

To see how this was understood and taught in the Indian experience, we must now consider in more detail the *Bhagavadgita*.

We have already noted that the setting of this great discourse is a fictitious one. But it is a fiction so appropriate that it must have been carefully chosen. It takes us back to a decisive moment in India's history, the great battle between the Kurus and the Pandavas. These were rival dynasties disputing the hegemony of India or at least a part of India. But although they were rivals, they were closely related. Duryodhana, leader of the Kurus, was cousin to Yudhishthira, leader of the Pandavas. The Pandava army was commanded by the great archer, Arjuna, a brother of Yudhishthira, and Arjuna had, as his charioteer, none other than Krishna, transported back (according to our chronology) about a thousand years. The *Gita* is a dialogue between Arjuna and Krishna.

I said that the fictitious setting on the battlefield was a very appropriate one. It was a situation of life and death, for before the battle was over, many of those who stood there in the contending armies would be dead. Such a situation naturally conduces to wondering about the meaning and purpose (if any) of our human existence. It was also a situation that raised grave moral questions, especially in the conscience of Arjuna. Because of the ties of kinship, he recognized the faces of many relatives and friends in the opposing army. He felt that he could not kill or injure them, and that any victory he might win would leave him without any desire to go on living. So he declares, 'I will not fight!' So this is the starting-point for the dialogue.

In may seem strange that Krishna, the messenger and embodiment of divine love, does not encourage Arjuna in his pacific intentions. On the contrary, he rebukes him for faintheartedness, dishonourable in a leader at a time of crisis. This apparent contradiction is only one of many in the *Bhagavadgita*, and though we may speak of these opposites as 'dialectic', it is hard for Western minds to understand it. Sometimes, for instance, Krishna seems to recommend abstinence from action or work (*karma*); then it appears that the work to be shunned is work when accompanied by desire or by attachment to the fruit of the work; again, it is suggested that what we assume to be our work or our action is not really ours at all but something that is working itself out in our lives without our control (something like *karma* in the sense of a fate); then work is understood also in a bad sense, rather as the Protestant Reformers condemned 'works-righteousness' as opposed to faith. This last point seems to be illustrated by the often-quoted verse (called in the school of

Ramanuja the 'last verse', because it was taken to be the end of the discourse and the summing-up of all the preceding teaching), 'Surrendering all the laws, come for refuge to me alone, I will deliver you from all your sins; have no care.'[11] This is the goal, when the soul is surrendered to God (Krishna) in complete *bhakti*, that is to say, loving devotion. This intimate relation of the soul to God is in itself the fulfilling of the law. It is no longer necessary to strive to fulfil the commandments, for they are transcended in this devotion to God. 'Give up in thought to me all that you do, make me your goal; relying on the integration of the soul, think on me constantly.'[12] Presumably when one has reached this stage of union with God, one need think no longer of the laws or strive to fulfil them, for such fulfilling flows from the relation to God. The laws are not abolished, but transcended. The renunciation of work is not worklessness or inaction, but work free from attachment, work performed without passion, work that is not greedy of its fruits. 'With soul detached from everything, with self subdued, all longing gone, renounce; and so you will find complete success, perfection, works transcended.'[13]

But we must not hurry on too quickly through this teaching. We now begin to see where it is leading, but we must go back to where we left Arjuna when Krishna urged him to go into battle, we must try to follow the thinking that led thence to the 'last verse' and the triumph of *bhakti* over the way of works. Krishna advances various reasons in urging Arjuna to fight. The first is that death is not the greatest of evils but simply part of the human condition. According to Krishna, all the human beings on that battlefield had existed from eternity and would continue to exist for all future time. During this endless existence, death occurs many times, as the soul leaves one body to assume another. This should not be a cause of grief, and in particular, it does not constitute a ground for avoiding battle. 'As a man casts off his worn out clothes and takes on other new ones, so does the embodied self cast off its worn out bodies and enters other new ones.'[14] A second line of argument is pursued by Krishna, this time that Arjuna's duty, as a member of the warrior caste, is to lead the people in war. We may wonder whether this is not equivalent to urging Arjuna to action, and we have already seen that Krishna does not think that the way of works will lead to salvation. But we saw also that there is an ambiguity here. The evil lies not in works as such but in the desires and ambitions that accompany them. None of us can avoid works, but they should be works not of our own choosing or for our own advantage, but the works laid on us by our place in the ordered scheme of things. Even Krishna has his work to do, and if he were not to do it, the world would fall into chaos. Now, part of the world order is the caste system, and it assigns to Arjuna his work as a *kshatriya* or warrior-leader, and if he were to shrink from this work, he too would be inflicting damage on the cosmic order.

To modern Western readers, the two arguments I have cited would seem very poor reasons for starting a war, but they do make sense in the context of ideas within which the *Bhagavadgita* has come into being. Both Krishna and Arjuna conduct their discussion on a basis of shared presuppositions, namely, the basic doctrines of the classical Indian philosophy. This means that they both accept that the soul is immortal and that it transmigrates at death from one body to a new one, and apparently Krishna thinks that this mitigates death as an evil. Both parties in the dialogue also accept the caste system as basic to the world order and this dictates the action which is proper to Arjuna in his situation.

It is important to remember that this legacy of belief lies behind the *Bhagavadgita* and is for the most part unquestioned. Krishna is not a religious innovator, starting from scratch, as it were. The new ideas and new ways that he brings are culled from within the system in which he has grown up and are expounded as compatible with that system or, at least, with its main features. The Western reader may be particularly perplexed by the acceptance in the *Gita* of the caste system. How is that compatible with the recognition that Krishna's message is a 'gospel of love'? It has to be said, first of all, that the religion of *bhakti* is open to all, irrespective of social class, sex, civil status. Krishna says: 'Whosoever makes me his haven, base-born though he may be, yes, women too and artisans, even serfs, theirs it is to tread the highest way.'[15] One has to say further that Krishna, beginning from a very rigidly stratified society, brought into it a glimpse of universalism which has gradually subverted many of the old injustices. Love has within it a power which, given time, eventually breaks down all barriers.

It is the emphasis on love and on the personal relationship that is the distinctive contribution of Krishna. These things were not indeed absent in the pre-Krishnaist religion of India, but now they were made fundamental. Of course, one could not say that Krishna represents Hinduism, for Hinduism is too vast and variegated a phenomenon to be represented by one individual or one school of thought. But with the rise of the Krishna cult, new emphases come to the fore in Hinduism. These can be seen in both the way by which the believer comes to God and in the conception of God himself.

Indian religion recognizes three ways to God – the way of works, the way of knowledge or contemplation, and the way of devotion (*bhakti*). We have already seen that Krishna has an ambiguous attitude toward work or action, for though there is work that demands to be done, we can easily be led astray by desire or by pride in achievement. Work always involves the body, and there is a stage beyond work, the way of knowledge or contemplation which brings, says Zaehner, 'an intuitive apprehension of the Absolute'. But in Krishna's teaching there is still a third and higher way, the way of personal love and devotion. This is the most intimate union of all.

But this exaltation of the way of love demands a reconception of the Absolute or the ultimate reality itself. This had usually been conceived in impersonal terms, a mystery beyond all names and distinctions. The Absolute might indeed have personal manifestations, but these were subordinate to or emanations from a reality more ultimate than themselves. Krishna reverses the order. If the way of love or *bhakti* is the highest way to God, then God himself must be a personal God for only persons are capable of standing in a loving relationship.

So Krishna's final word – and that means God's final word – is: 'I love you well. Therefore will I tell you your salvation. Bear me in mind, love me and worship me, sacrifice, prostrate yourself to me: so will you come to me, I promise you truly, for you are dear to me.'[16]

It is not hard to understand why this message of a loving God became so influential in India especially after the long and somewhat arid period that preceded it. But there is still a problem remaining, and something has to be said about it. In chapter 11 of the Gita, Arjuna asks a proof, as it were, of Krishna's divinity. He asks to see him in his full reality. Krishna consents, and is transfigured into his 'highest sovereign form'. It is a 'form with many a mouth and eye and countless marvellous aspects, a God whose every mark spells wonder, the Infinite facing every way. If in heaven should arise the shining brilliance of a thousand suns, then would that perhaps resemble it.' Is this vision of overwhelming power and majesty not something less than the 'pure unbounded love' of which we have been hearing?

To this criticism it might be replied that a religion of pure *bhakti* is in some danger of becoming merely emotional or sentimental; and further that God, though not less than personal, may well have dimensions of being that are not exhausted by our concept of personhood. If God is God, then he must compel our worship as well as our love. There must be an element of the numinous in God. Perhaps this was part of the Dravidian contribution to the figure of Krishna, and perhaps it is preserved in the theophany of chapter 11.

Whatever we may decide about these matters, the reader will remember that after he was struck by the hunter's arrow, Krishna died, but not before he had granted absolution to his killer. The tradition tells us that after breathing his last, he rose all radiant and ascended to heaven where he was greeted by the gods. I do not think we can grudge him a place among the mediators.

8

Jesus

(7 BCE–33 CE)

The reader will have noticed that in giving dates for the persons and events discussed in this book, I have used the notation BCE (Before Common Era) and CE (Common Era), rather than the traditional BC (Before Christ) and AD (Anno Domini or Year of the Lord). The change makes no difference to the fact that the birth of Jesus Christ is still the central event in relation to which historical time-reckoning is calculated the world over, but the substitution of CE for AD makes the Western way of dating events more acceptable to non-Christians, who may indeed accept that this is the year 1995, but for whom it is not the Year of the Lord. But it is not just for politeness' sake that one makes this change. The exact dates of Jesus' life are still uncertain, but it is virtually certain that he was not born in the year 1, as traditionally supposed. This date was calculated by a churchman called Dionysius Exiguus in the sixth century, but he was several years out. Two of our four Gospels place the birth of Jesus in the reign of Herod the Great (Matt. 2.1; Luke 1.5). Now Herod died in 4 BCE. If one used the BC/AD notation, one would have to say that Jesus was born at least four years before Christ, which is absurd. So in the interests of good sense, it is better to use the BCE/CE way of referring to dates. The chronological questions concerning the birth of Jesus are very complicated, and we have no need to go into the details. At present, scholarly opinion favours a date about 7 BCE.[1]

The stories which Matthew and Luke tell about the birth and early childhood of Jesus are more legendary than historical. At the time when it happened, the birth of this child would attract no attention outside of the family circle. The Gospels were written from seventy to a hundred years later, when the once obscure child had become the Mediator acclaimed by Christians, and to them it seemed obvious that his birth must have been marked by special happenings, such as the appearance of a bright star in the sky, or the singing of a host of angels. Doubtful too is the place of Jesus' birth. When people became interested in the circumstances of his birth, he was already believed to be the Messiah expected by the Jews, therefore he must be a descendant of King David, and must have been born in David's city, Bethlehem. But Jesus himself seemed to disclaim Davidic ancestry (Mark 12.35–7). It is more likely that Jesus was born in the town in which he grew up, Nazareth, and he was commonly called Jesus of Nazareth.

Jesus spent his childhood in the family of Joseph and Mary.[2] Joseph appears to have been a carpenter (*tekton*) – a word which means a worker in wood or, more generally, any skilled craftsman (Matt. 13.55). It is quite probable that Jesus himself learned the trade, for when he returned on a visit to his home town in the course of his ministry, the people asked: 'Where did this man get all this? What is the wisdom given to him? What mighty works are wrought by his hands? Is not this the carpenter, the son of Mary and brother of James and Joses and Judas and Simon, and are not his sisters here with us?' (Mark 6.2–3). A skilled craftsman was a respected member of the community, and when people of modern times sometimes speak of Jesus as a 'Galilean peasant' they are not merely being contemptuous but are wide of the mark.

However, in the pages of the Gospels, we never encounter Jesus at work as a carpenter. According to Geza Vermes, 'The New Testament record leaves no room for doubt that during his ministry Jesus practised no secular profession but devoted himself exclusively to religious activities.'[3] (The word 'religious' in this quotation does not refer just to prayer and worship, but includes healings, exorcisms, teaching, fellowship meals, pastoral ministry in the widest sense.)

So where did Jesus get all this, to come back to the question asked by the people of Nazareth? Here we are confronted with the phenomenon of what are called the 'hidden years', the thirty years or more between Jesus' birth and the beginning of his public ministry. Quite early in his ministry, we hear that 'they were astonished at his teaching, for he taught them as one who had authority, and not as the scribes' (Mark 1.22). He is sometimes addressed as 'Rabbi', not because he held any ecclesiastical office but because of the intrinsic character of his teaching. This could only have come about as a result of long study and preparation during these hidden years. Jesus' teaching, and likewise his skill in controversy, shows that he had received a good education. Josephus tells us that there was care about education in first-century Palestine, especially in religious knowledge. It began in the family, was continued in elementary school, then in the synagogue, and gifted pupils might go on to study in the school of some rabbi.[4] We know nothing of the details of Jesus' education, but he must have had some training like that which Josephus describes. The story told by Luke of Jesus at the age of twelve discussing with the doctors in the Jerusalem Temple may be a legend, but it could well be based on someone's reminiscence that from an early age Jesus had devoted his energies to the study of his nation's religious traditions. This reminds us again that the mediators whom we are studying were not usually founders. They built upon traditions that were already there. Jesus has become known to us through the Christian church, but he was himself a Jew, and certainly in his lifetime thought of himself as working within the Jewish faith for the benefit of the Jews. He is reported as saying: 'I was sent only to the lost sheep of the house of Israel' (Matt. 15.24).

Apart from the isolated incident of the youthful Jesus in the Temple, the canonical Gospels are silent about him until he commenced his public ministry. Here we have to take note of another religious figure of the time, John the Baptist. According to Luke's account, John was about six months older than Jesus, and a fairly close relative. John had adopted the life-style of some of the early Hebrew prophets. He lived in the desert, away from the towns and villages, leading a simple ascetic existence. He may have been associated with the Essenes or with the Qumran community. His preaching was strongly marked by apocalyptic ideas, namely, that the end of the age was imminent, that divine judgment was shortly to take place, and that men and women must repent and turn away from sin if they were to escape the anger of God. Many people flocked to John and were baptized by him for the forgiveness of sins. Among them was Jesus. Whether this meant that he became for a time a disciple of John is uncertain, but Jesus' experience at his baptism in Jordan was a deeply decisive one. 'When he came out of the water, immediately he saw the heavens opened and the Spirit descending on him like a dove; and a voice came from heaven, "Thou art my beloved Son; with thee I am well pleased"' (Mark 1.10–11). After the baptism, Jesus spent forty days fasting in the wilderness, tempted by Satan. After that, he went into Galilee, 'preaching the gospel of God, and saying, "The time is fulfilled, and the kingdom of

God is at hand; repent, and believe in the gospel"' (Mark 1.14–15). To begin with, therefore, his message was very similar to John's. But the two men soon diverged. Jesus did not follow the ascetic discipline that John had embraced; and whereas John had retired into the Judaean desert, Jesus frequented the towns and villages, associating with all sorts and conditions of people, including those on the very fringes of society.

Although the Gospels represent the relation between Jesus and John as a friendly one and also claim that some of Jesus' earliest disciples had been previously followers of the Baptist, there may well have been some rivalry between the two groups. Certainly, as we have noted, the two leaders went about their work in quite different ways. Both encountered opposition. In Jesus' own words, 'John came, neither eating nor drinking, and they say, "He has a demon"; the Son of Man came, eating and drinking, and they say, "Behold, a glutton and a drunkard, a friend of tax-collectors and sinners!"' (Matt. 11.19). The way of the religious reformer is hard, a veritable no-win situation.

But it seems that Jesus' early ministry did awaken a response among many ordinary people. Mark's Gospel, in its early chapters, stresses the healing miracles which he performed, and which were one of the signs looked for in the promised Messiah. There can be no doubt that Jesus did have a gift for what is called 'spiritual healing', and the phenomenon still occurs today. It is a phenomenon not well understood, and it is said that the healings often prove to be only temporary. The Gospels simply testify that Jesus did in fact heal people suffering from a variety of conditions, and this brought him a considerable following of supporters. There is also mention of nature miracles, such as walking on water (Mark 6.45–52) and turning water into wine (John 2.1–11). Such stories cannot be taken literally, and indeed Jesus made it clear that he did not seek to persuade people to believe his message by such means. But stories like the two I have mentioned can have far more significance as parables or allegories, than if we take them literally.

How long Jesus went about in the course of his ministry is uncertain. The first three Gospels can be interpreted as implying that the ministry lasted only for a year. John's Gospel seems to imply at least three years, and perhaps it went on even longer. The chronology is disputed, and the evidence is not clear. Luke tells us that John began his preaching 'in the fifteenth year of the reign of Tiberius

Caesar, Pontius Pilate being governor of Judaea' (Luke 3.1). He also says, 'Jesus, when he began his ministry, was about thirty years of age' (Luke 3.23). Pontius Pilate became governor in 26 CE, and the fifteenth year of the Emperor Tiberius was three years later in 29. That would seem quite a reasonable estimate for the beginning of John's mission. But where does this leave us with respect to Jesus? Even if he was among the first to be baptized by John (we do not know if he was, but it is possible), then, since we accepted a date of 7 BCE as quite probable for his birth, he must have been thirty-six in the year 29. I suppose one might say, 'He was about thirty', meaning simply that he was a man in his thirties. But making Jesus considerably older than thirty eases the problem with regard to another piece of chronological information, this time from John's Gospel. In the course of a controversy with some Jews, they say to Jesus, 'You are not yet fifty years old' (John 8.57). According to some scholars, fifty was a significant age among the Jews – one became a *presbus*, a word usually translated 'old man', but as it was meant in this case to be honorific, perhaps we should say nowadays, a 'senior citizen'. The remark would be strange if Jesus were only 'about thirty' but much more natural if he was about forty, as he would be if we accept the 7 BCE date for Jesus' birth and the Johannine belief that his ministry extended over three years.

So far we have noted that a wide range of pastoral activities was characteristic of Jesus' ministry. Alongside this must be set his teaching. That teaching had many parallels in the sayings and writings of other Jews – indeed, Vermes says of Jesus that when 'the essential features of the Gospel report are inserted into the context of contemporary political and religious history, Jesus of Nazareth takes on the eminently credible personality of a Galilean Hasid'.[5] To make this comparison is in no way to deny the power and originality of Jesus' teaching which is still in modern times an inspiration to many people.

Much of Jesus' teaching on the ethical side is concentrated in what is called the 'Sermon on the Mount'. This is not so much a 'sermon' as a collection of moral sayings and discourses which Matthew has brought together. It has been suggested that in placing these sayings in the context of a sermon given on a mountainside, Matthew implies a comparison between Jesus and Moses at Sinai. Jesus is the new Moses, and he is giving the new law. But the new law does not contradict or supersede the old law, though it deepens the old law and makes it more inward. As W. D. Davies has said, 'not antithesis but completion expresses the relation between the law of Moses and the teaching of Jesus'.[6]

First come the 'Beatitudes' (Matt. 5.1–10), a series of sayings in which certain groups of people are pronounced 'blessed'. This sets the tone for what follows, for the blessed are not the rich and powerful or those who enjoy esteem, but the humble and meek:

Blessed are the poor in spirit, for theirs is the kingdom of heaven.
Blessed are those who mourn, for they shall be comforted.
Blessed are the meek, for they shall inherit the earth.
Blessed are those who hunger and thirst after righteousness, for they shall be satisfied.
Blessed are the merciful, for they shall obtain mercy.
Blessed are the pure in heart, for they shall see God.
Blessed are the peacemakers, for they shall be called sons of God.
Blessed are those who are persecuted for righteousness' sake, for theirs is the kingdom of heaven.

Those who hear and follow this teaching are said to be the 'salt of the earth' and the 'light of the world'.

In the next section of the 'sermon', we come to the antitheses, sayings in which Jesus quotes an old law and then gives it a new and deeper interpretation (Matt. 5.17–48). A few examples will suffice:

You have heard that it was said to the men of old, 'You shall not kill'. But I say to you that every one who is angry with his brother shall be liable to judgment.

You have heard that it was said, 'You shall not commit adultery'. But I say to you that everyone who looks at a woman lustfully has already committed adultery with her in his heart.

You have heard that it was said, 'An eye for an eye and a tooth for a tooth'. But I say to you, do not resist one who is evil. But if anyone strikes you on the right cheek, turn to him the other also; and if anyone would sue you and take your coat, let him have your cloak as well.

You have heard that it was said, 'You shall love your neighbour and hate your enemy.' But I say to you, love your enemies and pray for those who persecute you.

The teaching goes on. There are warnings against hypocrisy and against any show of piety. There are warnings too against repetitious prayers that do not get beyond words. Jesus teaches his disciples what is the best-known prayer in the world, and is appropriately known as 'The Lord's Prayer' (Matt. 6.9–14):

Our father who art in heaven,
Hallowed be thy name.
Thy kingdom come.
Thy will be done,
On earth as it is in heaven.
Give us this day our daily bread;
And forgive us our trespasses,
As we forgive those who trespass against us;
And lead us not into temptation,
But deliver us from evil.
For thine is the kingdom, the power and the glory,
For ever and ever. Amen. (*Book of Common Prayer* version)

There is much more in the Sermon on the Mount, and one should study also the somewhat different version of these teachings given in Luke's Gospel. We can well understand that those who heard this teaching were astonished, and we can understand why the people of Nazareth asked, 'Where did he get all this from?'

Of course, questions are bound to be asked about the practicability of Jesus' teaching. If, for instance, everyone started turning the other cheek, would this not lead to a breakdown of law and order? And can one control desires and emotions, in the way he seemed to demand? Jesus does not abolish the law of Moses, but he goes beyond it and sets before us more 'strenuous commands'.[7] Some say they are impossible demands, not to be taken literally but to be borne in mind and interpreted in varying situations. Others have tried to take them literally, in the belief that though they will always be held by a minority, they will nevertheless help to bring about changes for the good in the wider society, like leaven in a loaf of bread, to allude to one of Jesus' own similes (Matt. 13.33). Still others, notably the New Testament scholar, Albert Schweitzer, have argued that Jesus taught an 'interim ethic', valid only for the supposedly short time that would elapse before the end of the age and the actual coming of the kingdom. But only a few have followed Schweitzer in this, and the prevalent opinion nowadays is that he exaggerated the apocalyptic or eschatological *motif* in Jesus' teaching.

There is also a large amount of teaching scattered through the four Gospels, apart from the Sermon on the Mount. Much of this teaching is given in the form of parables. In these, Jesus tells a brief story, drawn from ordinary scenes of daily life, and uses the story to bring home to his hearers some truth concerning the spiritual life of men and women. Many of these parables are meant to elucidate Jesus' key conception of the kingdom of God. Mention was made of one of them in the preceding paragraph. 'The kingdom of heaven is like leaven which a woman took and hid in three measures of flour, till it was all leavened' (Matt. 13.33). In the same context, Matthew includes another brief parable of the kingdom: 'The kingdom of heaven is like a grain of mustard seed which a man took and sowed in his fields; it is the smallest of all seeds, but when it has grown, it is the greatest of shrubs and becomes a tree, so that the birds of the air come and make nests in its branches' (Matt. 13.31–2). Famous is the parable of the Good Samaritan, in which Jesus redefined the notion of the 'neighbour'. My neighbour is not necessarily the person who lives next door or someone to whom I am related, but anyone in need whom I can help, even a person of an alien or hostile race (Luke 10.25–37). Equally famous is the parable of the prodigal son (Luke 15.11–32).

We have been dwelling on the teaching that Jesus gave during his ministry, and before that we glanced at his pastoral activities in healing, exorcism and the like. Are there any other events from this period that throw light on Jesus and his mission? I shall mention three. The first is Jesus' choice of twelve men (presumably representing the twelve tribes of Israel) to be his lieutenants, as it were, and to exercise responsibility among the larger body of disciples (Mark 3.13–19). This may be seen historically as preparing the way for the Christian church, though whether Jesus himself saw it in this light is doubtful, especially if he was expecting the new age to break in very soon. The second point is the recognition of Jesus by the disciples as the Messiah or Christ. According to Mark, followed in this by Matthew and Luke, it was Peter who, in answer to Jesus' own question, 'Who do you say that I am?' replied, 'You are the Christ!' (Mark 8.27–30). Some students of the New Testament, including the greatest one in the twentieth century, Rudolf Bultmann, believed, however, that Jesus was hailed as the Messiah only at a later time, not during his ministry. This may have been due to the fact that the Messiah, believed to be promised in the Hebrew scriptures, was usually conceived in triumphalist terms as one who would literally restore the kingdom of David, and that was something very different from the kingdom which Jesus preached. The third point is the event known as the transfiguration. Jesus took three of the twelve apostles, Peter, James and John, to the top of a mountain. There they were joined by two figures from Israelite history, Moses and Elijah. Jesus was transfigured before the apostles and shone with brilliant light (Mark 9.2–8). No doubt this visionary experience was an event in the consciousness of the three followers of Jesus, rather than an objective historical event, but it did signify a critical moment in their thinking about Jesus, summed up in the words: 'This is my beloved Son; listen to him.'[8]

Jesus had, on the whole, been well received during his ministry, but it was not the idyllic experience which romantic imagination has sometimes represented it to be. There were critics and even enemies, and much of his teaching was given in the context of sharp controversies. Somewhat surprisingly, the Gospels tell us that the sharpest exchanges took place between Jesus and the Pharisees. This is surprising because the Pharisees were serious-minded men, who were seeking to reform and deepen the faith of Israel. One might have expected them to support Jesus. Some of them did, but this was not generally the case. The Sadducees, the party of the ecclesiastical establishment, were almost natural enemies, and probably they would have opposed any free-lance teacher who was not subject to their authority. The opposition to Jesus gradually hardened, and he must have been aware of it, even if we think that the predictions of his sufferings in the Gospels owe more to the hindsight of the evangelists than to actual utterances as he approached the end. It is possible that, even quite late in his ministry, Jesus might have crossed the Jordan into the sparsely settled territories to the east, and been safe from his enemies. But that would have meant the abandonment of his life's vocation, and I suppose we would never have heard of him. Instead, he resolved to go up to Jerusalem.

Why did he go up to Jerusalem? Looking back after an interval of several decades, the evangelists believed that Jesus had gone up to Jerusalem as part of God's pre-ordained plan for the salvation of mankind. Perhaps that is true, but it is not an explanation that I feel able to put forward in this book. As Christian and a priest, I want to believe that. But I am trying in these chapters to put forward as faithfully and impartially as I can accounts of nine great mediators of the spiritual life, and in order to do this, I try to confine myself to facts and hypotheses which are open to any of my readers, and to suspend from consideration such judgments of faith as that 'God was in Christ reconciling the world to himself' (I Cor. 5.19). I think that in fact we can offer a probable and sufficient (though inevitably speculative) explanation of Jesus' decision to go to Jerusalem, while confining ourselves to purely human and historical realities. Jesus went to Jerusalem with human hope in his heart. His mission must be carried to the very heart of the Jewish establishment, and he must have hoped that he would get an affirmative response. But the hope was not a blind one. He knew very well that Jerusalem had a reputation of killing the prophets. He knew too that his former ally, John the Baptist, had been executed by the authorities. Luke quotes him as saying, 'O Jerusalem Jerusalem, killing the prophets and stoning those who are sent to you!' (Luke 13.34). I am saying that, as a human being who can see only a limited way ahead, Jesus did not have a full knowledge in advance of what would happen when he got to Jerusalem. But he knew enough to be aware that death was a definite possibility. His death invites comparison with that of Socrates. In both cases, it becomes integrated into the person's life, as the high point of his vocation and mission. It is no accident that the narratives of Jesus' passion and death occupy so much space in the Gospels, for all the teaching that he had given, the beatitudes and the Sermon on the Mount, the parables and all the rest now found concrete expression in Jesus' last hours, so that some writers have described his life and death as an acted parable.

Arrived in the neighbourhood of Jerusalem, Jesus seems to have lodged outside the city with friends in the village of Bethany. That he had friends in and around the city suggests that he had been there before and supports the Johannine chronology of his ministry.[9] In fact, when he went into the city proper, he was greeted by a group of enthusiastic supporters who received him apparently as Messiah. He then went on to the Temple and drove out some hucksters who were trading in the sacred precincts, selling small animals for sacrifice and exchanging currencies. These events were probably on a very small scale, and cannot be interpreted as a political rising, as Reimarus tried to do. However, scholars differ in their estimates. John Knox tends to minimize them, while E. P. Sanders thinks they were more serious and triggered the action of the authorities against Jesus.[10]

The great Jewish festival of the Passover was approaching,[11] and Jesus arranged with one of his friends in Jerusalem that he would celebrate the Passover meal at his house.[12] In this 'Last Supper' with his disciples, Jesus, according to the Synoptic Gospels and also Paul, instituted the Christian eucharist, a sacrificial meal in which Christ and his death are commemorated, just as the deliverance from Egypt had been commemorated in the Jewish passover. In the history of the Christian church, there have been many controversies over the precise significance of the eucharist, but across all the differences of theology this rite has remained as the central act of Christian worship. It is the way in which Christ is called to mind and the worshippers still realize a sense of his presence.

After the meal, Jesus and his band (now reduced to eleven, because one had gone over to the enemy) retired to an olive grove on the Mount of Olives. The traitor Judas brought the Temple police to the spot, Jesus was arrested and taken away for trial. The story of the trial itself is difficult to disentangle. Two jurisdictions were involved – the Jewish and the Roman. The precise nature of the accusation is not clear – the Jews seemed to be concerned about blasphemy, but this was not important to the Romans, whose concern was political. They could hardly help interpreting Jesus' talk of a 'kingdom' as indicating a political ambition to overthrow Roman rule, and would hardly be likely to understand Jesus' protestation, 'My kingdom is not of this world' (John 18.36), even if these words are historical. So Jesus was condemned to death by the barbarous method of crucifixion, and the sentence was carried out at once. Although one cannot be certain about dates, the chronological scheme for which I have argued in the earlier parts of this chapter would point to 3 April 33 CE, as the likely date for the crucifixion, Jesus being then about forty years old. Why bother about dates? I think C. H. Dodd answered that question. Though he favoured a date three years earlier, he wrote; 'All lines run back to that precise point which we may date tentatively to Friday, 7 April, AD 30. Not indeed that the exact calendar date is either certain or important; other dates are possible between AD 29 and 33; but it *is* of some importance that the church remembers an event which is actual, concrete and in principle datable like any other historical event.'[13] The Apostles' Creed makes the same point when it inserts the words 'under Pontius Pilate' after the mention of Jesus' suffering. The point is simply that Jesus and the other mediators were not products of mythology or visitors from some heavenly region beyond this earth, but human beings who lived and suffered and achieved in real history, and who may therefore be acclaimed as 'stars in the human sky'.

The body of Jesus was taken down from the cross by his disciples and reverently placed in a tomb. That should have been the end of the story. The authorities had planned well; let this agitator be destroyed, and his movement will die with him, for there is no one among his followers who can take over the leadership. But that was not how things turned out. The story got around that Jesus had returned from the dead and was still active among his disciples. The evidence for this was pretty weak. Some women who had visited the tomb reported that they had found it empty. There could be many explanations for that. Some of the disciples had experiences in which, as they believed, they had seen Jesus alive and heard him speak. They may have been suffering hallucinations. But whatever one says about such stories, the small company of Jesus' followers did not vanish from history. It seems that at first they scattered; they did seem to believe that this was the end of it all. Then they came together again, they believed fervently that Jesus was still with them. And out of this came the Christian church and the Christian message, still with us today. Whatever we may think of the idea of resurrection, the historical fact that cannot be denied and has to be explained is that Christianity would never have come into existence apart from the conviction that Christ was risen.

There is a well-known passage from Tacitus,[14] quoted in almost every textbook on Christian origins, which *may* contain an unconscious allusion to the resurrection or alleged resurrection of Jesus. I have not seen this interpretation advanced anywhere else, but if it is correct, then Tacitus would be the only early pagan writer to allude to the historical problem to which 'resurrection' in some sense would be a solution. After mentioning that the Emperor Nero had fastened the blame for the great fire in Rome in 64 CE on the Christians, Tacitus, writing about the end of the first century, explains to his readers who the Christians are. He has obviously a low opinion of them:

Christus, from whom the name [of Christians] had its origin, suffered the extreme penalty during the reign of Tiberius at the hands of one of our procurators, Pontius Pilatus, and a deadly superstition, thus checked for the moment, again broke out not only in Judea, the first source of the evil, but also in the City [of Rome] where all things hideous and shameful from all parts of the world meet and become popular.

This talk of Christianity being 'checked' by the execution of Jesus and then 'breaking out' again conforms exactly to the New Testament accounts of the crucifixion and resurrection. This might be called the objective or historical phenomenon to which 'resurrection' might be a solution. But how 'resurrection' is to be understood is a problem which I do not think lies within the scope of this book. No doubt the concept could be understood in many different ways. Also, there is no doubt that in all the mediators we have considered as well as Jesus, there was something eternal and indestructible that has brought new life to succeeding generations of disciples.

9

Muhammad

(570–632 CE)

'Muhammad is very close to us – we love him and respect him.' These words, reported recently in a leading English newspaper, were uttered not by some authoritative figure in Islam, but by a star in the world of sport, the famous Pakistani cricketer, Imran Khan. I quote his words not only because it is unusual nowadays for a prominent sportsman to speak so positively and publicly about a religious leader, but because his words show us the tremendous attraction which Muhammad still exercises more than thirteen centuries after his death. In an age when we seem to have moved into a 'twilight of the gods', the religion which looks to Muhammad as its mediator has been experiencing new vigour, though this has perhaps manifested itself more in the political than in the strictly spiritual field. The attraction of Muhammad may in part be due to the fact that he has always been an unmistakably human figure, even a very earthly figure, and neither he nor his followers made any claim that he was divine. Yet at the same time he inspires among these followers a very profound reverence as the one who has opened for them a way to God. Alongside the words of Imran Khan, the twentieth-century disciple, we may set those of Abu Bakr, Muhammad's most faithful follower in the earliest days, and eventually his successor as the first caliph. Abu Bakr's daughter, Ayesha, became Muhammad's favourite wife. When Abu Bakr was called to Ayesha's apartment and learned that Muhammad had just died at the age of sixty-two, he addressed the dead leader in these words: 'Thou art my father and my mother, O Apostle of God, most sweet in life, most sweet in death.'[1]

Who then was this Muhammad who could evoke and can still evoke such powerful responses? He was born in about the year 570 CE, in the city of Mecca in Arabia. Muhammad had a difficult start to life. His father died before he was born, his mother died when he was just a few years old. The orphan was then entrusted to a grandfather, who also died, and left the boy to be brought up by an uncle. Muhammad's social position was not an exalted one, but neither was it one of deprivation.

The city of Mecca had two noteworthy features. It was, first, an important trading centre, located on a busy caravan route that led from the south of Arabia to Syria in the north, with branch routes going off to Egypt, Persia and other regions. It was, second, an important religious centre. Mecca, like some other cities in Arabia, possessed a shrine to which pilgrimages were made by people from all over the peninsula. The shrine was (and still is) a cube-shaped building, known as the Kaaba. In the wall of the building is set the famous Black Stone, an object of veneration which may have been a meteorite that had descended from the sky. Also, in Muhammad's time, there were some images associated with the Kaaba. One was of the god Hubal, and though it is uncertain, it may have been Hubal who was simply called sometimes 'The God'. In Arabic, this would be *al ilah*, which is contracted to Allah, the word which Muhammad and his disciples have used for God. But when Muhammad was born, other divine figures also had their images in the Kaaba precincts, particularly the goddesses Al-Lat and Al-Uzza, who may have been wives or daughters of Allah. So the religion was polytheistic, though even before Muhammad's time, paganism may have been on the wane in Arabia as it was elsewhere. There were in fact considerable numbers of both Jews and Christians living in Arabia at that time.

Such was the environment in which Muhammad grew up. Not surprisingly, he found employment in the caravan trade, at first assisting his uncle who was engaged in that trade. Muhammad was apparently successful in his work, and about 595 he was hired by a wealthy widow, Khadija, to take charge of a caravan proceeding to Syria. Muhammad fulfilled his duties so well that the widow made him an offer of marriage, which he accepted.

Presumably he spent the next fifteen years or so in caravanning around Arabia and the neighbouring countries, and must have met many new people and probably picked up many new ideas. He must also have developed habits of thought and meditation, and it is said that he frequently went out to a cave in the vicinity of Mecca to spend time in prayer and contemplation. He was forty when he had his first revelation. The archangel Gabriel appeared to him and said,

Read, in the name of thy Lord!
Who created man from congealed blood.
Read, for thy Lord is most generous!
Who taught the pen.[2]

The nature of this revelatory experience is not quite clear. The opening word could mean either 'read' or 'recite'. The passage quoted is included in the Koran, and according to one tradition, Muhammad had a vision of the Koran incised in stone. Although he had never learned to read, one may suppose that he believed that God had 'taught [him] the pen', so that he was able to decipher the writing. Another tradition claims that when Muhammad was having a revelation, it was like the sound of a bell to begin with, and then gradually resolved itself into words. Perhaps both traditions describe his experience. He may have had a vision of the archangel Gabriel and of the written text, while the voice of the archangel revealed to him the meaning of the writing.

It seems that Muhammad was not expecting a revelation. On the contrary, he was frightened by what had happened, and wondered if he was going mad, or if he was being mocked by some malevolent jinn. (In Arab folklore, the jinn were spirits of the desert, some good and some bad.) He told Khadija about his experience and the doubts that were troubling him. She restored his courage and assured him that he had really received a message from God. So Muhammad came to believe that God was indeed calling him to a mission.

The first revelation was followed by many others, and the sum of these constitutes the Koran ('recital'), the sacred book of Islam. Like most of our mediators, Muhammad did not claim to be a founder or innovator. It is therefore an error to call the religion which he taught 'Muhammadanism'. He believed that he was teaching a religion that had existed from the beginning of history, the religion practised by Abraham, who is ancestor supposedly of Jews and Arabs alike. The religion he was called to teach was, he believed, a proclamation to the Arab people of the religion that had been revealed in the beginning, and that religion is Islam ('submission' [to God]) and those who believe in it are Muslims ('those who submit'). So Muhammad had no difficulty in calling Moses and even Noah, Muslims.[3] This is a parallel to the claim of Justin Martyr that Socrates and Heraclitus were 'Christians before Christ'.[4]

The Koran had existed in heaven graven on stone tables from all eternity. The only novelty in the case of Muhammad was that now the eternal truths were being imparted to Arabs by their own Arab prophet, just as truth had been revealed through Moses to the Jews, through Zoroaster to the Persians, through Jesus to the Christians, for each nation has its own prophet. 'Thus we have sent thee to a nation before which other nations have passed away, to recite to them that with which we have inspired thee.'[5] The foundational truth in the revelation is that there is no God but the one God. He has no partners or associates. For this reason alone, it would be absurd to talk about a 'Muhammadan' religion, for all true religion is Islam, submission to God alone.

As to the Koran itself, although it was or is an eternal text, it was communicated to Muhammad section by section, God telling him that he has divided it up and sent it down piecemeal, as occasion required.[6] The many parts, called *suras*, were collected after Muhammad's death by his secretary, Zaid. The secretary, however, paid no regard to chronological order, but placed the longest *suras* first, then the shorter ones, and this results roughly in a reverse chronological order. Thus the first revelation, quoted above, does not appear until Sura 96 (out of 114). From what has just been said about the Koran, it will be understood that Islam is almost bound to be fundamentalist. This follows from the idea of an eternal unchangeable text. Even translations of the Koran are not acceptable, but only the Arabic text, for a translation can hardly avoid making changes in the meaning.

We can pass fairly quickly over the years in which Muhammad's new religious movement was taking shape in Mecca. He began to make converts, including his own wife Khadija and also Abu Bakr, mentioned above. This Abu Bakr was one of Muhammad's most zealous converts, and was also the person chiefly responsible for spreading the Muslim faith. He did this discreetly by approaching persons whom he knew and trusted, so that to begin with Islam was a kind of secret society.[7] But it was impossible to keep it secret indefinitely, and as news of the movement leaked out, it aroused strong opposition among the Meccans. This was inevitable, as Muhammad's teaching struck at the religion of the Kaaba. There was some mild persecution of the Muslims, but Muhammad's uncle was able to protect him from serious trouble. Nevertheless, as time went on things became more difficult for Muhammad and his followers. It is presumably to this period that there belongs the legend of how Muhammad, rejected by the Meccans, preached to the jinn of the desert. Some of them became Muslims, and confessed, 'we have heard a marvellous Koran that leads in the right direction'.[8]

The Koran is relatively free of myth and legend, but to this Meccan period there belongs the most famous legend of all connected with Muhammad, that of his night journey to Jerusalem. This may have been originally a visionary experience of Muhammad which then got worked up into a legend. It is only fragmentarily reported in the Koran. 'Celebrated be the praises of him who took his servant a journey by night from the Sacred Mosque (the Kaaba) to the Remote Mosque (the site of the Jerusalem Temple), the precinct of which we have blessed to show him of our signs.'[9] Muhammad, having flown through the air on his horse to Jersualem, ascends up into heaven and learns there the proper forms of worship.

But let us return from legend to history. It was about this time too that Muhammad made contact with some men from Yathrib, who had come to Mecca on pilgrimage. (Yathrib was the old name for the city which became known as Medina or Al-madina, which means simply 'the City', that is to say, 'the City of the Prophet'.) Muhammad found these people from Yathrib more receptive to his teachings than the Meccans, and after further contacts, the Muslims resolved to forsake Mecca and move to Yathrib. The migration took place over a period of several months in the year 622 CE. This event, called in Arabic the *hijra*, marks the beginning of the Muslim calendar. In Western texts, Muslim dates are given with the designation AH, an abbreviation of the Latin *anno hegirae*, 'year of the migration'; for instance, the Muslim year 1400 AH fell in the Western year 1979 AD (or CE). The apparent discrepancy which arises when one adds 1400 years to 622 and come up with the answer 1979 is due to the fact that the Muslims reckon by lunar years, normally of 354 days.

So began the new era, and before long it began to look as if Muhammad and his faith would be unstoppable. Muhammad's first act at Medina was to arrange the building of a mosque (*masjid*, 'place of prostration').[10] Round it were built living quarters for his wives (Khajida had died before he left Mecca, but the prophet eventually had ten wives, and lived in their quarters without a house of his own). The mosque was the venue for the daily prayers. These prayers, known as the *salat*, were said at five times during the day. They had been said in Mecca in secret, but now they could be said openly. It must be from this time that the call to prayer, one of the most characteristic features of Islam, had its beginning. One of Muhammad's earliest followers, Bilal, a former slave who had been purchased and manumitted by Abu Bakr, was the first muezzin or summoner to prayer. He would climb to some eminence (there were as yet no minarets) and from there he would call the people. That call eventually took a form which amounted to a kind of basic creed of Islam, and has been used by Kenneth Cragg as the basis for an exposition of the whole Muslim faith. In its current form the call runs:

> God is most great, God is most great. I bear witness that
> there is no god except God. I bear witness that Muhammad
> is the Apostle (*rasul*) of God.
> Come ye unto prayer.
> Come ye unto good.
> Prayer is a better thing than sleep.
> God is most great, God is most great.
> There is no god except God.[11]

To begin with, it appears that prayers were said facing toward Jerusalem, but after Muhammad's quarrel with the Jews, they were said facing Mecca. The institution of Friday as a special day of prayer also seems to date from this time, and likewise the fast during the month of Ramadan.

We have seen that Muhammad claimed that Moses had been a Muslim and that he claimed to be in the tradition that had stemmed from Abraham. Thus in the earliest days of his mission, he had tended to see the Jews as allies against the pagan Meccans. Perhaps Muhammad's thoughts on monotheism had been first aroused by contacts with Jews on his caravan travels. When he settled in Medina, he found quite substantial Jewish communities living in the area. But these Jews, to his disappointment, did not hasten to embrace the Muslim mission. On the contrary, some of them were critical of Muhammad, pointing out that many of the references in the Koran to incidents in the Hebrew scriptures were inaccurate. Muhammad replied by complaining that the Jews had tampered with the scriptures. This was obviously absurd, but, along with other factors, it contributed to a falling out between Muslims and Jews. Some of the Jews were expelled, others were killed, and the seeds were sown of that conflict between Judaism and Islam that has lasted

down to the present day, though indeed it goes back to an even
earlier antagonism between the Israelites and the desert tribes.

But the Jews were not Muhammad's only enemies, or even the
most dangerous. The Muslims had left Mecca because the majority
of the people there were opposed to their religious innovations, and
soon the hostility of the Meccans was increased for more practical
reasons. The Muslims had been welcomed by their friends in Medina
and had been helped to settle in their new home, but they could not
live in dependence on these people indefinitely, and had to find a way
of supporting themselves. The way which Muhammad chose was
that of raiding caravans, which had to pass near Medina on the route
leading north from Mecca. It may seem surprising that a religious
leader would choose such a course, but we have to remember that
outside the few cities, Arabia was in Muhammad's time a pretty
rough part of the world, and raiding caravans was not a sin in the
eyes of the Bedouin of the desert. Muhammad shared that view, not
so much because of a lax morality, but because for him religious
commands override moral duties. This is a dangerous doctrine, but
we must remember that it has had its advocates also in the West,
notably Kierkegaard. For Muhammad, the overwhelming reality in
his life was the mission to which, as he believed, he had been called by
God himself. Nothing, not even the common rules of morality, could
be allowed to stand in the way of that mission. Aggression, whether
against Jews or against Meccans, was justifiable. As Margoliouth has
expressed it, 'the use of the sword had been divinely authorized'.[12]

Is there an element of fanaticism here? This is a question which we
leave aside for the moment, but it is certainly too important to be
swept under the carpet, and we shall have to return to it.

The policy of raiding caravans brought at first only meagre results,
for these caravans were well protected. But then Muhammad took a
further step in the 'teleological suspension of ethics', if we may use
Kierkegaard's phrase. He decided to attack a caravan during the
'sacred months', a period when there was observed among the Arabs
a kind of 'truce of God'. At such a time, people went about unarmed,
for violence was taboo. Presumably Muhammad knew that his
action would be regarded as sacrilege, but since he had rejected the
old paganism, its precepts were no longer binding for him. But he
must have been troubled in his conscience, for he found it necessary
to produce a revelation to vindicate his action: 'They will ask thee
about war in the sacred month. Say, war therein is a great sin, but to

turn aside from the cause of God, and to have no faith in him and in the Sacred Mosque, and to drive out his people [from Mecca] is a worse sin in the sight of God.'[13] It can hardly be denied that Muhammad now thought of himself as an absolute authority, above the laws that governed ordinary men and women. It is true that he did not claim a divine status, but he thought of God's apostle as so close to God himself that in practical terms the difference hardly mattered. 'It is not for a believing man or a believing woman to have any choice in a matter, when God and his Apostle have decided about it.'[14]

In any case, the Muslim raiders set out in the sacred month, intercepted a Meccan caravan, and brought back rich spoils. In 624 they attempted to repeat the exploit by waylaying a caravan commanded by Abu Sufyan, a leading citizen of Mecca who from then on was the most important foe of the Muslims. On this occasion, the caravan slipped past the raiders, then Abu Sufyan reappeared on the scene with an army of perhaps eight hundred or a thousand men. The Muslims numbered only a little above three hundred. It seemed therefore to be a hopeless situation for Muhammad and his followers. There followed the Battle of Badr, and although the number of combatants involved was negligible compared with such modern battles as Waterloo or Alamein, this Battle of Badr must nevertheless be reckoned among the decisive battles of world history. If Muhammad had lost, we would never have heard of him and there would never have come into being the world religion of Islam. But contrary to all expectations, Muhammad did not lose. He and his followers put to flight the Meccan army. The victory is celebrated in a sura of the Koran in which God, in answer to a prayer of Muhammad, says, 'I will assist you with a thousand angels, with others in reserve.'[15] Muhammad had often been taunted by opponents, who said that he had never performed a miracle. But now he was able to point to the Battle of Badr as a miracle, for how indeed could three hundred men have defeated a force three times as large as their own, except their leader had been able to enlist an invisible battalion sent down by God himself?

Sporadic warfare between the Muslims and the Meccans continued for several years. In the year after Badr, a punitive expedition from Mecca encountered the Muslims at Uhud. This time victory went to the Meccans, and Muhammad himself was wounded, having two teeth knocked out by an arrow. But the Meccans did not follow up their advantage, and went back to Mecca. The Battle at Uhud did not become so famous as the Battle of Badr, but from the point of view of world history, it was equally significant. If the Meccans had pressed on to Medina, or if the arrow that knocked out the Prophet's teeth had followed a slightly different course, both Muhammad and Islam would have disappeared almost without trace. There was another confrontation in 627. Again a large Meccan force descended on Medina. This time Muhammad did not come out to do battle, but he had prepared a trench round Medina, and this seems to have proved too much of an obstacle for the attackers, who soon dismantled their camp and retreated to Mecca.

Meanwhile Muhammad and his followers were constantly gaining in strength, and in the next episode in the struggle with Mecca, they were able to take the initiative. In 628 Muhammad announced that he would make the pilgrimage to Mecca and set out with a numerous company. He did not actually enter the city, but came to an arrangement with the Meccans, according to which there would be peace between them for ten years, and that in 629 Muhammad would be permitted to make the pilgrimage. He did so, and in 630 he again set out for Mecca, this time with an army said to number ten thousand. The Meccans realized that there was no point in further resistance. Muhammad entered the city. One of his first actions was to enter the precincts of the Kaaba and to destroy the idols. So he fulfilled his ambition of establishing monotheism and putting an end to idolatry, which he regarded as the worst of all sins. Kenneth Cragg comments: 'This tremendous breaking of the idols, dramatized by the physical cleansing of the central sanctuary in Mecca after its conquest, was the supreme achievement of Islam.'[16] But a scarcely less dramatic moment must have been one that followed soon after when the original muezzin, Bilal, ascended to the roof of the Kaaba and the Muslim call to prayer resounded over Mecca. Abu Sufyan himself made his submission to the faith that he had opposed so strenuously. Muhammad treated his former enemies in Mecca with generosity, unlike the severe and even cruel treatment that he had meted out to the recalcitrant Jews of Medina. But after a short stay, he returned to Medina and continued to reside there.

Soon after the capture of Mecca, fighting broke out again. This time it was initiated by Bedouin tribes, who were unhappy with the new order in Arabia. They fought stubbornly but were subjugated, and in the final years of his life Muhammad became master of all Arabia and Islam was entrenched as the faith of the Arab people. Whether Muhammad himself visualized the spread of Islam beyond the borders of Arabia is debatable, but he certainly left the Muslim faith poised, as it were, for further conquests.

In 632 Muhammad presided at the pilgrimage to Mecca. He had wisely not abolished this ancient pilgrimage, not even the veneration of the Black Stone, but he purged it of pagan associations and incorporated it into the fabric of Islam. After the pilgrimage, he went back to Medina, but within a few weeks he contracted a fever and died in the apartment of his favourite wife, Ayesha, the daughter of Abu Bakr, as mentioned near the beginning of this chapter.

The centre of Muhammad's theology is unquestionably his doctrine of the one God. The doctrine is encapsulated in an early sura:

> Say, 'He is God alone!
> God the eternal!
> He begets not and is not begotten!
> Nor is there any like him!'[17]

This God is utterly transcendent, distinct from the creation and even from the human creation. But he is not just cold or impersonal. Every sura of the Koran is introduced by the phrase, 'In the name of the merciful and compassionate God'. It is also said that God is closer to a man than his own jugular vein. Muhammad's conception of God has affinities with both the Jewish and Christian conceptions of God, and historically they all have a Middle Eastern origin. But they have certainly drifted apart. Islam could not find room for such notions as the Christian doctrines of Incarnation and Trinity. Yet, as we have seen, Muhammad considered himself so close to God as the Apostle that it becomes hard to see a difference between a word of God and a word of Muhammad. Furthermore, almost every religion as it develops in history divides up into branches or sects and these must have sprung from some seeds latent in the original teaching, even if they have also been encouraged by external influences. For instance, most religions have produced mystics, though these are only a small minority. The stark monotheism of Muhammad and the emphasis on transcendence appear to be incompatible with any mysticism. Yet within Islam there appeared Sufi mysticism, perhaps not without the influence of Buddhism. But there may be a hint in those verses of the

Koran that speak of God's nearness. He is not just the stern ruler and judge, acting on human beings only from above and from outside. C. R. North claims that 'the Sufis arrived at their conclusions in their own way, and by beginning from Muslim premises'. He quotes a woman Sufi named Rabia: 'O God! If I worship thee from fear of hell, burn me in hell! If I worship thee in hope of paradise, exclude me thence! But if I worship thee for thine own sake, withhold not from me thine everlasting beauty!'[18]

The monotheism of Muhammad is definitely an ethical monotheism. God is the lawgiver, and an action is right if it is commanded by God, wrong if he has forbidden it. The term *sharia* is used for the corpus of law derived from the Koran as its primary authority. No distinction is made between religious laws and laws which regulate individual or political activity. This has caused difficulties in modern times due to the fact noted earlier that the Koran is an unchanging text. Such a text may have been applicable to human society in the time of Muhammad himself, it may even have seemed progressive when compared with what had gone before it. But severe problems arise when there is an attempt to apply it to societies of the twentieth century, hence the political conflict between so-called 'fundamentalist' Muslims and other Muslims who may be quite devout but who also accept that the state is a secular institution and its laws cannot be derived solely or even principally from religious sources. Some of the traditional laws would seem to demand penalties that are too severe by modern standards. An example would be stoning to death for adultery, which to Westerns or Westernized Muslims of the present day would be intolerably severe. On the other hand, some Muslims would reply that the West has become too lax in questions of sexual morality, or, indeed, that it has gone soft over a whole range of questions. But while Islam punishes (or might punish) some sexual offences severely, Westerners might complain that the treatment of women in Islam does not properly recognize their human dignity. But Muhammad has the credit of abolishing the cruel practice of burying alive unwanted female children.

Wars and violence are other areas of human conduct where there would be disagreement between Muslims and many non-Muslims. We have seen that Muhammad himself used force in propagating Islam in the early days, and the policy was continued by his successors. Even today, some zealous Muslims talk of the *jihad* or holy war against unbelievers, though moderate Muslims tend to allegorize this concept as symbolically expressing the struggle against evil. However, one may ask whether the attachment to peace and the quest for non-violent ways of settling conflicts, common in the teaching of many religious leaders, have been adequately represented in Islam. Another factor here that may make it difficult for Islam to come to terms with the contemporary world is the very literal way in which some Muslims practise the imitation of Muhammad, even in matters that have no moral significance. For instance, they try to shave precisely in the way that Muhammad is supposed to have used.

It is very important, however, not to become onesided in trying to understand Muhammad's views on society and human conduct. If he was severe in some matters, he was kind and generous in others; we have seen, for instance, that he was generous towards his old enemies at Mecca, and he commanded almsgiving and care for the unfortunate. If he believed in punishment for wicked deeds, he also said, 'If ye punish, punish [only] as ye were punished'[19]; this is something like a minimal version of the so-called Golden Rule. There are many other affirmative points in Muhammad's moral and social teachings. Margoliouth points out that 'the freeing of slaves was one of the earliest acts of charity imposed on those Muslims who could afford it'.[20] The tradition also claims that he strove for a more compassionate treatment of animals.

No system of ethics is perfect, and Muhammad's is not an exception to this rule. What is even more difficult is living according to one's ethical principles, and here we may say that Muslims have possibly been more zealous in trying to live up to their principles than Christians. One has also to say that if fanaticism and violence have had their place in the history of Islam from Muhammad onwards, they have also been evident in other religions and seem to be peculiar temptations to all who hold seriously to a religious faith, even when they contradict the authentic teaching of that faith.

Finally, we may notice that for Muhammad, God is not only the giver of the moral law, he is also the ultimate judge of human action. Sometimes in the Koran we find the expression, 'belief in God and in the Last Day', almost as if these two conceptions were of equal importance. Muhammad did believe that human actions find their proper reward, be they good or be they bad. His pictures of heaven and hell are vivid and imaginative, and cannot be taken at all literally. But they express a deep conviction that nothing is more ultimate than our moral choices.

Conclusion

I have headed this final chapter 'Conclusion', but I should say right away that it will be a very tentative conclusion. I visualize that inter-religious dialogue will go on for a long time yet, and what the end of it will be it is impossible to say, since we are thinking of a living relationship that is in the process of unfolding and the end of which cannot be foreseen. The very fact that the dialogue is taking place gives good grounds, I believe, for the hope that the end will be affirmative and life-giving for all the religions, for a dialogue aiming at increased understanding has reversed the former state of affairs in which the several faiths lived in rivalry with one another. But when one has got beyond the rivalries, what is the prospect? Surely not a gloomy merging of all those rich traditions with their varied histories into some nondescript generalized 'natural religion', that would kill off all the particularity and concreteness of the actual existing religions. But it would seem to be equally unsatisfactory to say, 'Let us preserve all the wealth of diversity in the separate traditions', for every religion seems to have in itself an impulse toward unity with the others. Especially in a world in which secularism and materialism are already dominant and set to become more so, the religions experience the need to draw together if the truths and values concealed in the vague term 'religion' are to survive and make their influence felt, an influence which will be for the good of all.

The task then is the exceedingly difficult one of somehow reconciling the quest for a more than superficial unity with a respect for the claims of concrete beliefs and practices that have already proved their worth over long periods of time. Perhaps it cannot be done at all – we have still to find that out.

In this book, we have confined ourselves to the limited task of studying in far too brief a compass some of the great religious leaders who have set in train movements and communities in which their insights have been further developed and sometimes, it must be said, corrupted. When we consider these leaders and try to understand what was essential in the contribution of each of them, we strike again this problem of unity and diversity, though in a simpler form from the one which it has if an attempt were being made to compare the developed systems that look back to these leaders.

I used the word 'mediators' to describe the religious leaders we have been studying. I defended the use of this word on the grounds that it has a broader range than some other words that might have been used, such as 'saviours' or 'saviour figures', 'prophets', 'revealers' and so on.[1] What seems to be common to all of them is that each one has mediated to a group of human beings a new or renewed sense of holy Being, which many call by the name 'God' or the equivalent term in other languages, but which many others designate, perhaps thinking that the word 'God' is too personal or too anthropomorphic or too closely connected with the many limited 'gods' of polytheistic religion, by other terms, such as the One or the Ultimate or the Absolute. Some of these mediators have been primarily teachers; others have been more than teachers in the sense that their own lives have been, so to speak, an acting out of their teaching; still others have engaged in political activity; but all have stressed the spiritual nature of human beings.

In the survey carried out in the present book, we have encountered mediators of several types. We must now try to analyse more closely the similarities and differences that we have found in these mediators – the family resemblances, to employ Wittgenstein's useful term. Not all of the mediators exhibited all the qualities that can belong to the mediatorial office, but we can discern across the differences a persistent type that we may call the type of the mediator.

The analysis will take place in several stages. First, we consider the mythological and legendary material that has gathered around these figures, and we shall find many recurrent themes in this material. Secondly, we try to isolate the historical careers of the mediators, and again we shall find recurring patterns, alongside wide divergences. Thirdly, we consider similarities and differences in their teachings. Fourthly, we turn our attention to what might be called the 'theology' of mediation, something that is already implicit in the mythology, history and teaching. After that, we shall look again at this difficult question of pluralism in religion and the quest for the unity of the human race.

1. Mythology and Legend

The mediators of the great religions all lived in earlier times, most of them in Jaspers' 'axial period'.[2] Both their own thinking and that of their disciples took place long before the revolution in ideas which we call the Enlightenment, a revolution that marks a sharp divide between premodern and modern times. All the mediators who have been considered in the preceding pages lived on the other side of that divide from ourselves, and so did their disciples for many centuries. The mediators need to be themselves mediated to us, and this secondary mediation is effected by the traditions that have grown up around each one of them – maybe thirty-three centuries of tradition since Moses, the first of our mediators, and about fourteen centuries since Muhammad, the most recent among them. Modern historical method can to a large extent identify those elements in the tradition which are mythological or legendary. Though these elements are not 'history' in the sense of a record of events that actually happened in the past, they are not on that account to be dismissed as of no value. They are ways in which the mediators of the mediators sought to show their significance as persons who open ways to the divine reality and who bring human beings to a new awareness of the spiritual depths of their own being. They often did this by representing the mediators as miracle-workers or the recipients of unique privileges beyond the human level, and they did this in spite of the protests of some of these mediators themselves that they neither could nor would authenticate their message by signs and miracles. These would only obscure what they really wanted to communicate. But their protests fell on deaf ears, and some, though not all, are presented in the tradition within a framework of the 'supernatural'.[3] As I insisted in the Introduction,[4] the very idea of a mediator demands that such a person be truly and fully human. Unfortunately, some of the traditions introduced docetic tendencies which suggested that some of these mediators were not truly human but temporary visitors, so to speak, from beyond our world of space and time. Such teachings are subversive of the very possibility of mediation, yet they are not just to be eliminated, but must be examined with sympathy and reinterpreted, if we are not to miss some insight that was trying to find expression.

As we consider some of these mythological or legendary elements, we can hardly fail to notice that very similar myths and legends occur in the traditional accounts of mediators living at different times and in different cultures. Although it is only too easy to underestimate the extent of travel and communication in the ancient world, it seems very unlikely that many of these similarities are due to borrowing. There are, for instance, parallels between stories told about the Buddha and stories told about Christ, and these have long been known to students of religion and have excited some speculation. Some of the same stories appear in different form in other traditions. I shall give plenty of examples in a few moments. Here it is probably enough to say that the origin of such stories lies deep in the human imagination. They appear and reappear at different times and places not because of borrowings but because humanity participates in a deep unity and shares certain desires and aspirations (as well, possibly, as illusions), that remain the same though widely sundered in space and time. Let us now look at some of these mythico-legendary accretions, and see how they recur in the traditions concerning our nine mediators.

(a) Birth stories   Stories which are obviously legendary are told about the births of the mediators. Most of them were in fact born in obscure circumstances, and did not become well-known until they had completed their work. Even then, little would be remembered about their early lives, and it was only after their deaths that biographical interest arose, though by that time the possibility of getting reliable information had become small. But because these men were held in veneration for their teaching and their holy lives, pious imagination felt obliged to provide what were regarded as fitting births for them. Several were supposed to be the sons of kings – such was the case with Buddha and Krishna, while Jesus was given a genealogy showing his descent from the greatest king of Israel, David. Sometimes it was claimed that there had been a virginal conception – so it was with Buddha and Jesus. In the case of Lao-zu, there was an extraordinary legend that he had been carried in his mother's womb for seventy-two years before birth, while in the case of Zoroaster there was a complicated legend about a stream of fire originating in heaven and following a tortuous course until it ended up in the mother of the sage. Even the rationalistic Confucius was claimed to have been attended at birth by supernatural spirits and dragons.

A point emerging from this myth-making tendency is that the figures of the mediators, though founded on real persons of history, have been worked over by the imagination of their followers. Sometimes this may have had the effect of throwing into prominence some feature of the mediator that had made a special impression. Sometimes it may be the case that the picture has been distorted. We might compare the process to what happens when a painter produces a portrait. Such a portrait is not just an unimaginative picture of the sitter as he would appear to the camera. It is meant rather to express what the artist considers most striking in his subject, what he has perceived as expressing the character of his subject as one whose character was sufficiently impressive to demand the artist's attention. We know, of course, that this is a dangerous business, and that sometimes the subject of the painting, or, more likely, his or her relatives, are very indignant about what the painter has produced. Obviously such distortions can arise also in the accounts of great religious figures of the past.

I have said that we have to make a sympathetic attempt to understand what the mythological and legendary elements in the religious traditions are trying to say. We have to bear in mind that these elements in the accounts of the mediators, though partly coming from the mediators themselves, are partly, and even primarily, derived from the experiences of those whom I have called the mediators of the mediators. When Bultmann introduced the term 'demythologizing' into the theological vocabulary, he correctly saw that a myth is as much an account of the myth-maker's experience as it is a description of anything that has given rise to the experience. For instance, the story of a virgin birth expresses the sense that something startlingly new has entered history, that human nature has, if you like, been reinvented. In the days of Buddha or Jesus, that is the kind of idea that might well have found expression in the story of a miraculous birth. But the danger is that if taken in a literal biological sense, the story not only conflicts with our modern understanding of these matters but defeats itself by removing the mediator from membership of the race of Adam.

(b) The legend of the wicked king   In the case of several of our nine mediators, the child is hardly born when he is threatened by forces of destruction, usually personified as a wicked king or ruler. In our earliest exemplar of a mediator, Moses, the king of Egypt has decreed that the male children of the Hebrew slaves are to be destroyed, and Moses has to be hidden. Sinister figures, probably representative of the old Iranian religion, threaten the life of the

young Zoroaster. The wicked king of Mathura seeks to destroy Krishna, who has to be conveyed out of the city to be reared among the cowherds. King Herod of Israel massacres the children of Bethlehem in an attempt to eliminate Jesus, and the Holy Family flee into Egypt. The similarities in these stories are striking, yet there is no need to suppose any borrowing. They are putting on record in legendary form the universal human experience that evil is entrenched in any society, and the mediator will probably find that when he comes to his own, that is, to his fellow human beings, they are not willing to receive him (John 1.11).

(c) Early signs of vocation   Most of the mediators began their active careers in middle life, say at thirty or forty. But in a minority of cases, notably Buddha, Krishna and Jesus, there was a moment in childhood when they were recognized, and sometimes a second moment when they clearly showed their vocation, to the discomfiture of their elders. After Buddha's birth the sage Asita came to the palace, and announced that the child would become a Buddha; when Krishna was a child, his foster-mother happened to look into his mouth, and saw the whole world contained within him; when the infant Jesus was brought to the Temple, the aged Simeon hailed him as Messiah. These are obviously legends. But further, when Buddha was still a child, he went missing at a country festival, and was found in a trance under a tree; when Jesus was twelve years old, he went missing while the family was returning home after a pilgrimage to Jerusalem, and was found in the Temple there in discussion with the scholars. The point of these two last stories is not so obvious. It is possible that they do originate in actual incidents in which the thoughtful meditative character of these young people was already showing itself; or the stories may have been told because those who eventually devoted themselves to Buddha or Jesus believed that already in childhood some sign of their significance must have been given.

One could go on adding to this list of legendary events which could be paralleled in the lives of several mediators – temptations, miracles and so on – but I shall pass over them and mention only a legend which concludes the careers of about half of our mediators, a final exaltation or ascension.

(d) Ascension into heaven   Although in the case of Moses the story of an ascension into heaven is very late and apocryphal,[5] it seems very appropriate that this commanding figure of the Hebrew

scriptures should have been honoured with such a legend. Krishna and Jesus are both said to have ascended into heaven after their deaths. Muhammad made an ascension into heaven, but with him the event took place in mid-career, on the occasion of his legendary visit to Jerusalem. Such stories are meant to affirm the final triumph of the mediator when they come at the end of his career, and whether they occur at the end or before it, they speak also of his acceptance with God. But the idea of an ascension is perhaps among all the legends the one that most plainly speaks of an event in the experience of the believer rather than in the biography of the mediator. To tell the story of the mediator's ascension is simply to acknowledge his Lordship and to express the believer's faith that he was indeed an emissary from God.

2. History

Our second main topic in this chapter is to look at those events in the careers of the mediators that may be considered historical, though it is not always possible to distinguish the historical from the legendary, and sometimes an event which may very likely be historical has been given a legendary colouring. But in history, as in myth and legend, we find similar patterns showing themselves in the lives of these religious leaders.

(a) *Vocation*   I use the word 'vocation' in its traditional sense as 'calling'. In the lives of these men, there was generally a moment when they experienced the call of God to take up what they believed to be their lifework. Such a moment might also be called 'revelation'. The person concerned had a new vision both of God and of his own responsibility under God. The revelation included a vocation, that is to say, it was not merely the communication of a new insight into God, but a summons to take up a task which the mediator understood as God's will for him.

We have seen that there were such moments in the lives of most of the mediators we have been studying. Moses at the burning bush learned the name of God, though it was the same God who had been worshipped by his ancestors; learning the name of God, however, implied or was conjoined with a mission to go back to his people and to liberate them from their enslaved existence. Zoroaster had a visionary experience by the river bank and believed he was caught up into the very presence of Ahura Mazda, who taught him what he must preach to the Persian nation. Buddha had his famous experience of enlightenment when in the course of a night he passed through the various stages that brought him to the four noble truths and the noble eightfold path; this experience sent him too in search of disciples and issued in his first sermon. In the case of the two Chinese mediators, there does not seem to be any record of a definite moment of vocation. This does not mean that they did not experience such a moment, and may be due only to the paucity of our information about them. But perhaps they simply grew into their vocations by gradual stages. Certainly, they had vocations, however they reached them. Even Socrates, whom I have included (rightly, I believe) in the series, though he was not a 'religious' figure in the same sense as the others, had his moment of vocation. He too had what I have described as 'virtually a revelation',[6] though he received it not directly but through the agency of his friend Chaerophon. It led him to believe that God (Apollo) had called him to a mission, and his faithfulness to the call eventually brought him to death. In the case of Jesus, the moment of vocation came at his baptism by John. He had a visionary experience: 'he saw the heavens opened and the Spirit descending on him like a dove', and this was accompanied by his hearing a voice from heaven, 'Thou art my beloved Son, with thee I am well pleased' (Mark 1.10–11). This was the beginning of his public ministry, and soon he was preaching that the kingdom of God was at hand. Incidentally, the vocation of Jesus illustrates the point made earlier that these moments of vocation, though facts of history, are often given a legendary colouring. In the oldest account of Jesus' baptism, the one quoted above from Mark, the vision and the voice from heaven are private to the experience of Jesus himself; by the time the Gospels of Matthew and Luke were written, the opening of the heavens, the appearance of the dove, and the heavenly voice had become objectified as publicly observable phenomena. Our last example of a revelation which was at the same time a vocation comes from the career of Muhammad. In his case, as the reader will remember, he heard a voice (and may also have had a vision of a book) as he prayed in a cave near Mecca. The voice bade him 'Recite!' (or 'Read!') and so began his mission as the Apostle of the one God.

So right across the spectrum we find these records of deep religious experiences which marked the beginning of a career of mediation. These are the moments when the mediators entered the stream of history, and are essentially 'historical' in contrast to the imaginative birth legends. It may also be of some interest to note that these experiences of vocation seem to have taken place when the subject had reached maturity – ages of thirty or forty are mentioned in some of the cases, and this almost certainly implies that there were 'hidden' years of quiet meditation and pondering before the critical experience came.

(b) Doubts and temptations   A second historical truth about the mediators is that all or most of them had moments of self-doubt, and temptations to abandon their vocations or to modify them in ways that would be less demanding. That there must have been such moments of wavering seems to be simply a corollary of human nature itself. In the traditional accounts, however, these moments are sometimes disguised or played down or transferred to the realm of legend. This tendency arises from the great veneration that is accorded to the mediators. But this is to do them a disservice. For only if they were truly and fully human beings and achieved what they did achieve within the conditions of human history could they be real mediators and provide real grounds for hope to other human beings. The moments of doubt are attestations that when we recall the work of the mediators, we are in touch with beings who knew suffering, weakness and temptation like ourselves, but who nevertheless faced them and gave hope that they can be overcome.

Let us once again pass in review the figures of the mediators, this time noting their moments of self-doubt. In his encounter with God at the bush, Moses raises difficulties right away. 'Who am I to do what is asked of me?' Buddha is from time to time confronted by Mara, the mythical personification of evil. When he has gained enlightenment, is that not enough? Why should he go and preach the doctrine to others, exposing himself to hostility? Socrates has to resist temptations, right to the end when Crito urges him to flee from Athens and save his life at the expense of his principles. Immediately after Jesus' baptism, he is tempted by Satan to choose easier and more popular ways of appealing to the people than the way which was finally to lead to the cross. When Muhammad had his first revelation, his reaction was to wonder if he were going mad.

(c) Conflicts   Those who have known some overwhelming religious experience and have felt themselves touched and called by God cannot refrain from communicating it to other people. Especially if

they see fellow human beings suffering from ignorance, poverty, oppression, disease and other evils, and feel themselves to have been somehow 'liberated', to have known what the religions call 'salvation' or 'wholeness', they feel an obligation to open the way to salvation to others. Perhaps they expect that what they have to communicate will be welcomed with open arms. But not so. When Moses went to the Israelite slaves and told them that Yahweh had sent him to deliver them, he may have expected that they would be overjoyed, but they were in fact sceptical: 'The Lord did not appear to you!' (Ex. 4.1). His subsequent relation with the people was a very troubled one – indeed, we noted that according to one theory, the murmurings and rebellions culminated in the murder of Moses. Zoroaster met with resistance from the supporters of the old religion, and tradition states that he was murdered by one of the priests of that religion. The stories of Socrates and Jesus are too well-known to need rehearsing again – both are remembered as martyrs who laid down their lives for things which they valued more than life. The enemies who opposed the mediators were not for the most part criminals. They were more likely to be pillars of their several societies. But they felt themselves to be threatened. The mediators, bringing as they did a renewed vision of religion and its significance for human life, were inevitably subversive of the existing state of affairs.

(d) Death   All of our mediators died, several of them as a direct result of carrying out their vocation. If someone says, 'So what? Surely everyone dies!', that does not take away the importance of stressing the point that these mediators died. They were human beings, and therefore subject to death. They were beings of flesh and blood and finitude, not angels or demigods or 'immortals'. Unfortunately, it has sometimes been thought that they could be honoured by detaching them from humanity. In the early days of Christianity, various heretics claimed that Jesus had not died on the cross, for he was, (they believed), not a man but some kind of demigod. Even to this day, Muslims believe that Jesus did not die on the cross, but an idol was crucified in his place.[7] But if that were true, his entire mediatorial significance would be destroyed. John's Gospel penetrated to the truth when Jesus is made to declare: 'I, when I am lifted up from the earth, will draw all men to myself.' The evangelist adds: 'He said this to show by what death he was to die' (John 12.32–3). All of the mediators died, all of them spoke out of the

human situation. Yet all of them have become life-giving spirits, bringing hope into that situation.

(e) Communities and scriptures   These mediators have all been dead for a long time, yet, I say, they are life-giving spirits and are still inspiring hope in human beings. I am not going to venture an opinion as to whether they still live on as personal beings in 'heaven' or in the presence of God, but I now want to draw attention to the fact that in very similar ways they made provision for the continuation of their teaching and their way of life beyond their own deaths. That provision was surprisingly uniform for all the mediators. It was twofold – a living human community, and a written body of scripture.

Most of the mediators gathered around them a few disciples who in most cases became the nucleus of a wider community. Communities soon develop institutions, and so eight of our nine mediators (the exception is Socrates) have eventually become the central figures in religions, nowadays numbering many millions of adherents. Confucius and Socrates attracted students whom they taught in a kind of seminar situation; Buddha and Jesus both had bands of disciples who were soon spreading the faith to others; from the beginning Muhammad had the support of Abu Bakr, a zealous missionary who eventually succeeded his master as head of the Islamic community. A living community of the kind described perpetuates the life and thought of the person whom they regard as their leader and inspirer. His actual words are treasured and passed on by the original disciples. A community of this kind is almost certain to add to the teaching of its founder, and may sometimes actually corrupt that teaching. Modern scholarship can go far to determine what is original and what is later development, but the impress of the teacher remains, and religious reformations are usually attempts to return to the supposedly pure origins.

One way which seems to have been virtually universal in keeping contact with the beginnings and ensuring that innovations did not wander too far was the production of scriptures. These have different degrees of authority in the different communities. Many of them have a 'canon' of scriptures taken to be authentic. It is a fact worthy of comment that, as far as we know, none of the nine mediators considered in this book wrote anything himself! The actual writing was left to the disciples, and usually they did not get around to the task until several decades or longer after the death of the founder. Scriptures are invaluable for our knowledge of the mediators, but can cause rigidity (fundamentalism, literalism) in the religious community itself.

3. *Teaching*

We come now to a third round of comparisons, in which will be examined side by side some of the basic teachings of the mediators. The topics to be considered are God (or the Absolute), the nature of a human being, the material world, the moral life.

(a) God or the Absolute The very word 'mediator' implies standing between two realities and relating them to one another. In the case of the religious mediators, the two realities are God on the one hand and human beings on the other. All our mediators taught something about God and sought to open a way to God. I am using the word 'God' here in a broader sense than the one which it usually bears. In the West, where religious thought has been influenced for centuries by the Bible, that is to say, by Judaism and Christianity, God has been conceived as a personal being. Now obviously some of the mediators we have considered did not believe in a personal God as the ultimate reality. When I say that I am using the word 'God' in a broader than usual sense, I am extending it to cover conceptions that might be more properly designated as the 'Absolute' or the 'Ultimate'. In some of my writings I have used the expression 'Holy Being' as a way of designating the final reality as conceived in any religion, whether in personal or suprapersonal terms. I believe John Hick uses the expression 'Holy Reality' in a similar way. He writes: 'It is possible to use the term "God" with the proviso that it remains an open question whether God is personal or non-personal, or both personal and non-personal in different aspects or as differently conceived and experienced. But nevertheless the theistic associations of the term are so strong that it is always liable to misunderstanding.'[8] He goes on to suggest various alternatives, such as the Transcendant, the Ultimate, the Divine, the One, the Eternal, the Real. I shall allow myself some flexibility in using these various terms, but the point is that the mediators all bring to us some alleged understanding of this ultimately Real, whether called 'God' or some other name.

But do they *all* do this? Is not Buddhism, for instance, atheistic? I agree that Buddhism (or, at any rate, Theravada Buddhism) does not teach belief in a 'God' comparable to the biblical God, but to say it is atheistic is quite misleading, for the word 'atheism' is like the word 'God' bound up too closely with Western ideas (particularly with the materialism that was popular in the nineteenth century) to be applicable to Buddhism. The religions, including Buddhism, conceive the Real in spiritual terms or at least as analogous to the spiritual. If, for instance, Nirvana is taken to be the Ultimate for Buddhism, it is not a personal God, but, as we have seen in an earlier discussion, it is so far from nothing that it must be esteemed the highest reality. In the same discussion, we took note of the notion of *Dharmakaya*, as an Ultimate beyond both the human and the divine. John Bowker claims, 'It is a fundamental mistake to explain away theism in Buddhism as though it is peripheral to the Buddha's insight or intention.'[9] He thinks that the atheistic interpretation of Buddhism was largely due to the prejudices of Western scholars. Taoism is another example of a religion whose Ultimate is not to be conceived as a personal God. Indeed, the Tao is so far beyond our comprehension that we can have no clear idea of it at all.

So although all the mediators had a God or an Absolute and wished to communicate this to their followers, there are very wide differences in the ways in which they thought of the numinous reality. Even among those who were theistic in a narrower sense, there were considerable differences. God the Father, as conceived by Jesus, is not obviously identical with Muhammad's Allah, though clearly both mediators believed that they were referring to the same deity, for they identified him with the God of the Hebrew scriptures.

(b) Human nature I suppose it could be affirmed that all the mediators held that the human being is a spiritual being, and that, among other things, such a being seeks communion with God or the Absolute. But having said that, we find that there are wide differences. Both of the great Chinese religions take an optimistic view of human nature. Human beings seek the good, and it is within their capacity to realize it. Some other religions have a doctrine of grace, that is, the belief that human beings are incapable of attaining salvation and that they need the help of God. This is a point, however, at which the developed religions may have reached a different belief from that of the mediators. Paul is the Christian teacher for whom grace is all-important, but this emphasis is not to be found so clearly expressed in Jesus himself. Some forms of Mahayana Buddhism lay a similar stress on grace, but the older

Buddhism and Buddha himself are believers in the autonomy of the human will and its power to achieve the good life.

Serious questions arise when we consider the ideals of humanity represented by different mediators. Buddha, Confucius, Jesus, Muhammad are all admirable, even inspiring, figures, and many of their disciples have, in their own lives, reproduced the virtues of the mediators. But these ideals are different from one another. A good Buddhist and a good Muslim are both admirable, but one cannot combine the two ideals. They are just different. There seems to be no single timeless archetype of humanity, such as Kant supposed there is. The serious questions raised by this fact concern the unity and solidarity of the human race. These questions will be addressed when we consider pluralism and its limits in the final part of this chapter.

(c) A third topic in the teaching of the mediators concerns *the status of the material world*. Whether Moses himself gave any thought to this question we do not know. But certainly the tradition that sprang from Moses, the religion of ancient Israel and the Judaism which succeeded it, made much of the idea that God is the Creator of all that is, and the stories of creation were placed at the beginning of the Hebrew scriptures when they were brought together. This doctrine of creation was, it seems clear, fully accepted by both Jesus and Muhammad, and so passed into Christianity and Islam. Since the creation was the work of God, then it must be good. An important consequence has flowed from this. Believing that the material creation is good, the followers of the Abrahamic religions have had no qualms about enjoying its benefits. The religions of the East, by contrast, have not had a doctrine of creation. In the teachings of Lao-zu and the Buddha, the material world comes about by a process of emanation or perhaps deterioration from the ultimate reality. It is therefore to be viewed with suspicion, or even shunned. Very important developments have arisen out of these fundamental divergences of attitude. The West has devoted enormous energies to science and technology, and has not been much attracted by ascetic life-styles – indeed, one must frankly say that it has been drawn in the direction of self-indulgence and the desire for possessions, and has regarded nature as a source of wealth, with little regard for its inherent worth and dignity. The East has had great respect for those who 'leave the world', and we noted that Lao-zu's teaching provided the foundation for an attitude of wholesome respect for the natural world.

(d) Prayer and worship   We could hardly speak of a 'religion' if it did not involve its adherents in prayer and worship. There are, of course, many kinds of prayer and many forms of worship, and we find that those whom we have called 'mediators' gave their followers some instruction in these matters and themselves engaged in them. Jesus, in response to a request from his disciples, taught them the Lord's Prayer. This is a very simple prayer of asking, and such a prayer accords well with the belief in a personal God. It is a prayer quite free from egocentricity, for the tone is set by the petition that God's will may be done and his reign be established. It is interesting to compare with this prayer what Socrates, perhaps the most rationalistic among our mediators, thought about prayer. 'When he prayed', Xenophon tells us, 'he asked simply for good gifts, for the gods know best what things are good'.[10] He would not pray for money or power or anything that might not be approved by the gods or that would degrade prayer to a self-seeking form of magic. In the religions of the further East, prayer more often takes the form of meditation than of asking, but these two need not be considered as opposed to one another. Meditation, as in Buddhism, purifies the mind of those desires which might lead people to ask for the wrong things, but meditation will also kindle desire and aspiration for what is in accordance with our deepest understanding of the holy Reality.

(e) Ethics   All the great world-religions, as distinct from more primitive types of faith, give strong ethical guidance, and this in turn has its roots in the teachings of the mediators. At first glance we may be struck more by differences than by similarities. On questions which are important for the modern world, such as abortion, sexual morality, capital punishment, even peace and war, there are differences among the faiths and even within particular faiths. For instance, Christianity insists on monogamy (at least, as an ideal) whereas Islam accepts polygamy (at least, as acceptable for some). Nations which embrace Islam and Christianity have a long history of warfare (though with many dissentients in modern times) whereas Buddhists and Taoists have striven (not always successfully) to eliminate war as an instrument of policy. But if we go back to the mediators themselves, we find that in spite of these differences among their successors, there was a large measure of agreement on certain norms that lie at a deeper level – for instance, reverence for human life, already implicit in Moses' teaching, the emphasis on righteousness (Moses, Confucius, Muhammad) and even on love

and compassion for all (Buddha, Krishna, Jesus). And in spite of the frequent lapses into war and violence, the religious vision of peace, shared by a majority among the world-religions and understood not just negatively as the absence of war and violence but affirmatively as solidarity and harmony on the spiritual level, has powerfully inspired many men and women and pointed our modern civilizations along paths that lead to fuller life rather than along those that lead to destruction.

The religions not only teach morality to their adherents but many of them hold that there is a moral government of the universe, and that the good or evil which men do will bring its own reward or punishment either in this life or in a life beyond death. Zoroaster may have been one of the first to formulate a doctrine of eschatology, involving ideas of judgment, heaven and hell, and that teaching was influential for Islam and possibly also for Christianity and Judaism, though there was nothing of the kind in the religion of Moses. In the East, the dramatic eschatological mythology does not seem to have made an impression, but the idea of *karma*, the working out of good and evil deeds in further existences, is a parallel in Hinduism and Buddhism. In Confucius there is a somewhat different conception of moral government of the world, for Tien or Heaven is a kind of impersonal Providence.

4. *Theology of Mediation*

We have now surveyed in outline some of the basic characteristics of the mediators, comparing the myths and legends that have grown around them, the actual histories of these men so far as it can still be reconstructed, and the teachings that they have given. We now come to the question of the theology of mediation. What is the profile, so to speak, of a mediator in religion? What are the status and functions that constitute someone a mediator? We cannot expect a precise answer to the question, for mediatorship is more like a family resemblance than a clearly defined type. We have found differences as well as resemblances among those who make up our group of mediators. There is no single list of say ten or twelve essential marks that would be found in any mediator. In one we might find seven or eight of these marks, in another we might want to expand the list to thirteen or fourteen. This could easily depend on the accidental circumstance that records of one of them had been better preserved.

Perhaps the first step in moving toward a clearer theology of mediation would be to look more closely at the differences. Are they irreconcilable, or can they be understood as differences of emphasis and included in a broader view of the matter?

The most fundamental difference is surely over the question of God or the Absolute – the very fact that I have to use both of these expressions shows us how deeply this divide runs. On the one side stand the personal conceptions of God – the still anthropomorphic Yahweh of Moses, God the Father in Jesus' teaching, the Allah of Muhammad, certainly not anthropomorphic but surely personal; and on the other side, the Dharmakaya (or possibly the Nirvana) of Buddha, the Vishnu hidden behind the figure of Krishna and manifested as a somewhat terrifying cosmic impersonal reality in the *Bhagavadgita*,[11] the Tao of Lao-zu, and the Tien of Confucius, all apparently impersonal or suprapersonal conceptions of the Ultimate. Incidentally, it makes a lot of difference whether one writes 'impersonal' or 'suprapersonal'. Generally, by 'impersonal' one implies a level of being below that of the personal, but 'suprapersonal' is a word that makes it clear one is indicating a reality beyond the personal.

As we have noted, personal conceptions of God are characteristic of the Abrahamic religions and their mediators, Moses, Jesus and Muhammad, while non-personal conceptions are predominant in the religions of the further East, those that look to Buddha, Lao-zu and Confucius as their inspirers. But there is a dialectic that suggests to us that these differences are not absolute. In the West, we find from time to time various indications of an impersonal way of thinking about God, while in the East personal ways of thinking appear. Beginning in the West, we note that Christian mystics have tended to impersonal ideas of God. A striking example is Meister Eckhart. He spoke of an 'essence' of God underlying the persons of the Trinity and (in this following Dionysius the Areopagite) of a 'Godhead beyond God'. He declared: 'Intellect that presses on is not content with goodness or wisdom or the truth or even with God himself . . . It can never rest until it gets to the core of the matter, crashing through to that which is beyond the idea of God and truth, until it reaches the *in principio*, the beginning of beginnings, the origin or source of all goodness and truth.'[12] Among theologians of recent times, Paul Tillich did not hesitate to speak of the 'transcending of theism' and claimed that 'the content of absolute faith is the

God above God.'[13] We can find parallels in some Western philosophers who, even if not explicitly Christian, were certainly in the Christian tradition. F. H. Bradley held that the very notion of personality implies finitude, so the Absolute (which he distinguished from God) cannot be personal.[14] In a different philosophical tradition, Karl Jaspers maintained that the notion of a personal God is, in his terminology, a 'cipher' for the inconceivable ultimate which he calls simply 'Transcendence'.[15] In Islam, we have noted how the utterly transcendent God was brought closer by the Sufi mystics. However, mystics in the Abrahamic religions have often been suspect in the eyes of the more orthodox. Eckhart had been accused of heresy when he died in 1329, fortunately before his views were condemned. Likewise the Sufis have been suspect by the majority of Muslims, the Sunnis, so called because they follow the *sunna* or 'beaten path' marked out by Muhammad himself.

When we turn to the East, we find the other side of the dialectic, the appearance of personal ideas of God in faiths that are predominantly focussed on a non-personal Absolute. We have studied the most striking manifestation of this in Krishna. Hinduism had always allowed both personal and non-personal ways of understanding the Ultimate, but with Krishna the personal came to the foreground, and although behind Krishna was hidden the non-personal cosmic figure of Vishnu, Krishna displaces him as the high God for at least a very large number of Hindus.

What has been said about the dialectic of personal and impersonal (or suprapersonal) can be paralleled in other contrasts. There is transcendence and immanence. Once again, Christianity, Judaism and Islam are ranged on one side, that of transcendence, while Buddhism and Hinduism have a very strong sense of the immanence of the divine. The case of the Chinese religions is not so clear. But sheer transcendence and sheer immanence alike would lead to something like a disappearance of the Holy, in short, to a kind of atheism. So again a dialectic comes into play. In Christianity the transcendent God of Judaism receives an infusion of immanence in the doctrine of the triune God who is Father, Son and Spirit. In Islam, however, the transcendence of God is if anything, enhanced in relation to Judaism. A further parallel appears in the dialectic between temporality and eternity. Ideas of God which stem originally from the Hebrew scriptures present a God who acts in history and even retains traces of anthropomorphism, while in the Eastern religions God dwells in eternity. But these generalizations turn out, on closer inquiry, to demand qualification. We have to say paradoxically that God is both within time and above time, and the two conflicting views remain side by side, each correcting the other.

What can we say about the mediators themselves in this sketch of a theology of mediation? Again we seem to come into an area of dialectic or even paradox. I have said earlier in this chapter that the mediators were persons peculiarly sensitive to God, perhaps chosen or sent or inspired by God to communicate to the human race some knowledge of him and of his will for his creatures. In previous chapters I have insisted on the full humanity of these mediators, and argued that if they were not truly and fully human, they could not be mediators. The mediator has somehow to belong to both sides of the divide in which he exercises his mediatorial function. The mediator is a human being, yet as a human being he is immersed in the Spirit of God ('a man of God', to use the language of the Hebrew Bible), and therefore to some extent to be understood in his relation to God. The common myths and legends that we have seen attached to the mediators show how a sense of their humanity could be weakened and obscured because of the reverence paid to them as emissaries of God. Some of our mediators, especially Socrates and Confucius, come across to us as simply gifted human beings. But many of the others come 'trailing clouds of (divine) glory'. Even Moses, when he came down from the mountain with the tables of the law, had his face shining with a supernatural light because he had been communing with God.

The best known theological conception of the relation between God and a mediator is the Christian doctrine of incarnation. 'God was in Christ' was the relatively simple formulation of Paul (II Cor. 5.19), but the idea was developed by later Christian theologians in sophisticated philosophical terms, and has continued to be discussed down to the present time. Some critics have argued that this doctrine presents an insurmountable barrier to any genuine dialogue between Christians and non-Christians. I think this would be true only if one took a rather literalist and fundamentalist view of incarnation. On that view, the incarnation is understood as a once-for-all occasion, and if this were so, then one would have to agree with the author of one of the Pastoral Epistles of the New Testament, when he claims that 'there is one God, and there is one mediator between God and men, the man Christ Jesus (I Tim. 2.5). If the second assertion of that verse is literally accepted, then this whole book has been a mistake.

But I do not think that the incarnation of the divine Logos in Jesus Christ was a solitary unrelated occurrence, totally unique. Rather, I see it (and here I am speaking as a Christian theologian and priest) as the culminating point of what God has been doing in all history. Here I take my lead from Athanasius, often regarded as an exemplar of orthodoxy. He related the incarnation to God's immanence in the world. There is a sense in which the whole cosmos embodies the Word or Logos. Why then should not the Word be embodied in a human being within the cosmos? He writes: 'The philosophers of the Greeks say the world is a great body; and rightly they say so, for we perceive it and its parts affecting our senses. If then the Word of God is in the world, which is a body, and he has passed into it all and into every part of it, what is wonderful or what is unfitting in our saying that he came in a man?'[16]

Though God is immanent in the world, he is not equally immanent in everything. To say that he is, would be pantheism of the crudest sort. He is specially immanent in those creatures which have a share in his own spiritual nature, that is, as far as our planet is concerned, in human beings, and Christians believe that, among human beings, Jesus Christ was the one in whom God was signally present. On this wider interpretation of incarnation, we can see that it is so far from being a barrier that it provides a very fruitful basis for dialogue between Christianity and non-Christian religions, in some of which we can discern something like an idea of incarnation. The most obvious illustration of this is the figure of Krishna and I did mention earlier an incipient dialogue on Christology-Krishnology.[17] I think we could also find scope for dialogue with some forms of Mahayana Buddhism, where the *bodhisattvas* resign their attainment of Nirvana in order to labour on earth for the salvation of mankind. Even with Judaism a dialogue on mediation and incarnation seems possible. The eminent Jewish theologian and philosopher, Abraham Joshua Heschel, claimed that the Hebrew prophets (including, I suppose, Moses) were not mere mouthpieces or transmitters for the divine word to human beings, but were sharers in the *pathos* of God, by which he meant God's deep inner yearning for his creatures.[18] This participation in the divine *pathos* is admittedly not to be simply equated with incarnation, but it does indicate a very intimate relationship. When one remembers that, on the other side, some

Christian theologians, notably Schillebeeckx, have used the idea of the prophet to elucidate the person of Christ, it is clear that there is plenty of material here for Jewish-Christian dialogue.

So I am suggesting that the idea of incarnation provides a good starting-point for a theology of mediation, but this could only be on the assumption that incarnation was not a singularity or anomaly in world history but is a constant characteristic of God's relation to his creation. There are, one may say, degrees of incarnation. Christians believe that in Jesus Christ there has taken place an incarnation of the divine Logos adequate to our human needs. But they should not deny that in varying modes and in varying degrees the same Logos has been present in other chosen human beings. So a study of the mediators or saviour-figures in the great religions is a part of theology and even a part of christology.[19]

5. *Pluralism and its Limitations*

'Pluralism' and 'multi-culturalism' are popular words at the present time, especially among those who consider themselves 'progressive'. Yet at the same time nations, races and religions are being thrown together, so that we are also conscious of the need for the unity of human beings, for a solidarity that will embrace the differences. Here we are concerned only with the religious aspect of this problem. There are no obvious or easy solutions. Sheer pluralism would seem to weaken the sense of unity and belonging, and to encourage the rampant individualism that is characteristic of modern Western societies. On the other hand, any moves toward uniformity seem to be destructive of the wealth of human cultures, languages, architecture, liturgies and so on. Somehow, in religion as in society at large, we have to find a way of developing a deeper unity without destroying what is of value in the several traditions.

A sheer pluralism will not do, the attitude which says religion is a private affair, one religion is as good or as bad as another, it is simply a matter of personal choice. This is to ignore differences and to avoid questions of truth and falsehood. It masks indifference and must bear some responsibility for the rise in our time of strange and sometimes harmful sects. Equally unsatisfactory is the syncretism which prematurely merges the different traditions and is in grave danger of becoming shallow and sentimental. At least, one may say, syncretism makes some effort to respond to the desire for unity, but it has not worked at the problem in sufficient depth.

I think there will need to be a long period of dialogue before we begin to see the shape of a future relation among the religions that will satisfy the competing claims of unity and diversity. But what is perhaps chiefly needed at present is a new openness and respect for one another among the adherents of the separate traditions. This should not lead to any lessening of one's commitment to that particular tradition through which the influence of the Holy has touched his or her life. A renewed study of the mediators, the nine (or more) bright stars in the human sky, can be a significant step in the way to the future of religion.

Appendix

1. Chronology

I have tried to be as careful as possible in suggesting approximate dates for the 'mediators'. The word 'approximate' has to be emphasized, but the need to place these mediators in the chronology of world-history cannot be ignored. The reason for this, as I have already said, is a theological one. A genuine mediator must be a human being, one of ourselves, not a supernatural being who only appeared to be human, and not a mere product of the mythopoeic imagination.

Some readers may think I have been too credulous in accepting much of the traditional material concerning these mediators. But this material is surely bound to be at least our starting-point, though it has also to be subjected to criticism. Sometimes it is not difficult to distinguish legendary or mythological material from what may be genuine historical memory. For instance, material that involves the supernatural may be set aside. Likewise incidents that occur in the stories of many mediators look like elaborations added by disciples who had decided that 'it must have happened this way'. Phrases like 'forty years old' or 'a hundred and twenty years old' which are simply ways of indicating maturity or a ripe old age, should not be taken too literally. On the other hand, when it is said that someone was seventy-seven years old when he died, this does not sound like a figure that has just been plucked out of the air, and is more likely to be a genuine reminiscence.

Perhaps one should not strive too officiously to sort out the strictly 'historical' from alleged accretions. After all, what is the 'historical' Jesus, or 'historical' Socrates? Not the series of events in time that belonged to the isolated individual. One has also to take into account the influences of that individual on others, and their reaction to him, even their perceptions of him; and in the case of anyone who really makes an impression in human history, these actions and reactions continue even after the person's death. They all belong to the historical phenomenon which we call Jesus or Socrates or whoever it may be. In some cases, it may happen that impressions that are made by someone are so important that the individual life from which they stemmed is obscured. For instance, a recent book with the title, *The Life of Moses*,[1] does not investigate questions about the historicity of Moses, the date of the Exodus, and so on. It is concerned with the 'life of Moses' understood as the 'biography of Moses' as found in the Yahwist tradition embodied in the Pentateuch. It is this literary composition that is investigated with great learning and thoroughness. Obviously, it must be connected in some way with the life of the man Moses who lived in the thirteenth century BCE, but the connection has become obscure. As the biography, according to the scholar who has written the book, comes from the time of the Exile, seven centuries after Moses' death, it cannot have much 'historical' value. At least, not in a narrow sense. But one could say that 'Moses' (or the Moses-event, to take a hint from New Testament scholars who talk about the Christ-event) is indeed a historical phenomenon, though far transcending the life of the individual who gave his name to it. Much further removed from the historical substratum is the famous allegorical *Life of Moses* by Gregory of Nyssa.

But here I come back to my point that such mediators as Moses or Jesus lose their significance if the link with datable history is finally cut. As far as Jesus is concerned, C. H. Dodd made the point very clearly. About the death of Jesus, he wrote: 'All lines run back to that precise point which we may date tentatively to Friday, 7 April, AD 30.' But he adds: 'Not, indeed, that the exact calendar date is either certain or important; other dates are possible between AD 29 and 33; but it *is* of some importance that the church remembers an event which is actual, concrete and, in principle, datable like any other historical event.'[2] Something similar could be said about Moses.

Before leaving the subject of chronology, I should say why I have given the dates for Jesus of 7 BCE to 33 CE, which is a departure from the usual dating, as also from Dodd's (though he does explicitly allow for any year between 29 and 33 for the crucifixion). If one is to adjust the birth to recognize that it took place in the time of Herod, then it must be put before 4 BCE, though exactly how much before we do not know; and if one is to adjust the date of the crucifixion to allow for three years of ministry, then the most obvious (though not the only way) to do this is to date it at 33 CE. Additional plausibility is given to these adjustments by the fact that they make Jesus somewhat older than the conventional dating. A New Testament scholar whose view is very close to my own is Paul Maier, who writes: 'Although the precise date seems still unattainable for the nativity, some further refinement within the range of 7 to 4 BC is possible, which would suggest 5 BC as the most probable time for the first Christmas. This time frame along with 3 April 33 for the crucifixion provides a very balanced correlation of all surviving chronological clues in the New Testament, as well as the extra-biblical sources.'[3]

Mention may be made of a still more radical revision of the chronology of Jesus' life by Nikos Kokkinos.[4] This writer claims that, according to Josephus, John the Baptist died in 35, and as his death preceded that of Jesus, the crucifixion is dated to 36, the latest possible date, as Pontius Pilate relinquished his procuratorship in that year. But the rest of Kokkinos' evidence is unsatisfactory – a claim that the star of the Magi can be dated by astronomy to 12 BCE, and that the 'forty-six years' mentioned in John 2.20 refer not to the time the Temple was being built but to the age of Jesus. It is comforting to think that history and archaeology are as much troubled by uncertainties as is theology.

2. *Spelling and Transliteration*

Of our nine mediators all, with the exception of Socrates, were Asians. They spoke Asian languages and, if either they or their followers wrote anything, they did so in one of the many scripts of Asia. Even Socrates, though he left no writings himself, spoke a language that was written in its own distinctive Greek alphabet, different from the Latin alphabet that is used in Western Europe and the Americas. Now, every religion or philosophy develops its own vocabulary, and some of its key-terms cannot easily be translated into other languages without the danger of losing their meanings. These terms therefore tend to be used even when the religion or philosophy is being discussed in another language. It would be hard to discuss Hinduism, for instance, without using words like *karma* and *samsara*. The reader will have encountered a good many of these foreign words in the preceding chapters, though I have tried to keep them to a minimum. But just as the meanings of these words are hard to express in other languages, so the very sounds themselves are not easily transliterated into a foreign alphabet or script. Readers who go on to other books on Buddhism or Islam or one of the other faiths may well find that some of the terms introduced in this book are spelt differently, and may even sometimes be hard to recognize. So I plan to explain briefly the principles on which foreign terms used in this book have been transliterated into the alphabet familiar to English readers.

There are no universally accepted rules for transliteration or spellings. Sometimes a foreign word has been used in English books for such a long time that it has virtually been adopted into the language, and even if the spelling would be faulted by modern scientific standards, the word has become so familiar that it would be pedantic and confusing to change it. I have not therefore attempted to be entirely consistent and have retained some old spellings that are so well-known that they have become standard.

Thus, in the chapter on Muhammad, I have used the traditional English spellings of Koran and Mecca, though in many modern books that try to be more faithful to the Arabic, one would find Qur'an and Makka. Likewise I have used the anglicized names Moses and Zoroaster, though if one were to reproduce the originals, they would appear as Mosheh and Zarathushtra.

Difficulties arise in the case of the two Chinese mediators, Lao-zu and Confucius. For many years Chinese words were transliterated into the Latin alphabet in accordance with the Giles-Wade system. Since 1958 that system has been gradually superseded by the Pinyin system. Most readers will be aware of this, for they now hear on television news about what has been going on in Beijing, say, instead of Peking. I have tried as far as possible to follow the Pinyin conventions, since I believe that all school children in China now learn Pinyin before they go on to the traditional Chinese characters and it will presumably in time displace the older system. But some words have become so familiar in English books that I have left them unchanged. An example is the word *tao*, meaning 'way' (and other things). In Pinyin, this has become *dao*. It should be noted, however, that even when the word is written *tao*, the initial letter should be pronounced like an English 'd', and so also in derivatives like Taoism and Taoist. Proper names I have given in Pinyin, with the old spelling in brackets where there might be a difficulty in recognizing the name. But Confucius and Mencius remain with their time-honoured Latin names, as these seem to have become thoroughly English.

A word should also be said about some of the terms used in Indian religion. The basic religious vocabulary in India has been drawn from the Sanskrit language, and many people are familiar with such words as *karma* and *bhakti*. Buddhism, however, used a related language, Pali, in some of its oldest scriptures. In the chapter on the Buddha, I have followed the example of many other writers in using the Sanskrit, rather than the less familiar Pali forms. Thus I have written *nirvana* rather than the Pali *nibbana*, *dharma* rather than *dhamma*, and so on. But I have made an exception to this rule in the case of the famous Buddhist text, the *Dhammapada*, which has for so long been known in the West by that name.

3. *Principal World Religions: Estimated Numbers*

Christianity	1,900,000,000
Islam	1,000,000,000
Hinduism	800,000,000
Buddhism	350,000,000
Confucianism and Taoism	200,000,000
Judaism	15,000,000
Zoroastrianism	250,000

These figures are based mainly on the *Encyclopedia Britannica Year Book*, 1995.

Notes

Introduction

1. Maurice Wiles, *Christian Theology and Inter-Religious Dialogue*, SCM Press and Trinity Press International 1992, p. 2.
2. *Union Seminary Quarterly Review*, 20/1, 1964, pp. 39–48.
3. W. M. Abbott (ed.), *Documents of Vatican II*, Herder and Herder 1966, p. 660.
4. Ibid., p. 662.
5. Hans Küng, *Judaism*, SCM Press and Crossroad Publishing 1992. The slogan is printed facing the title page.
6. It should be noted that the conditions which make it impossible for anyone to pronounce an objective judgment that one religion is superior to another likewise make it impossible for the 'liberal' to say that all religions are equal.
7. H. R. Schlette, *Towards a Theology of Religions*, Herder & Herder 1966, p. 101.
8. Friedrich Hölderlin, *Selected Verse*, Penguin Books 1961, pp. 79–80.
9. John Macquarrie, *Jesus Christ in Modern Thought*, SCM Press and Trinity Press International 1990, pp. 415–22.
10. F. D. E. Schleiermacher, *On Religion*, Harper 1958, p. 241.
11. Some philosophers and theologians, from John Dewey to Don Cupitt, have denied that there is any reality called 'God' but have claimed that religion is still possible, though the word 'God' is to be understood as no more than the sum of human values. I very much doubt whether religion, be it Christian or non-Christian, would survive for long on such a subjective basis. Perhaps for a few academics it could still inspire hope and hold out a vision of peace and justice, but for most people it would have utterly lost its power. As John Hick remarks, a non-realist

religiousness 'offers welcome news for the few, which is at the same time grim news for the many' (*An Interpretation of Religion*, Macmillan and Yale University Press 1989 p. 207). I think that the few who would welcome the news that there is no God must be very few indeed.

12. Karl Jaspers, *The Origin and Goal of History*, Routledge 1953, pp. 1 ff.

13. I have adopted the official Pinyin system of transliteration for the name Lao-zu, often spelt Lao-tsu. See the appendix on 'Spelling and Transliteration'.

14. When the scribes brought before Jesus a woman allegedly 'caught in the act of adultery', we are told that 'Jesus bent down and wrote with his finger on the ground' (John 8.6).

1. Moses

1. W. O. E. Oesterley and T. H. Robinson, *A History of Israel*, vol. 1, Oxford University Press 1932, p. 70.

2. J. B. Pritchard (ed.), *Ancient Near Eastern Texts*, Princeton University Press 1955, pp. 483 ff.

3. The outline of Moses' career given here and the quotations are taken from Ex. 1–20 and Deut. 34. The approximate dates are based on the article 'Chronologie des alten Testaments' in *Das grosse Bibellexikon* (Brockhaus 1987), vol. 1, pp. 231–40.

4. See above, p. 7.

5. For a discussion of the significance of this name, see my *Principles of Christian Theology*, SCM Press and Macmillan 1977, ch. 5.

6. E. W. Nicholson, *God and his People*, Oxford University Press 1986, pp. 164–178.

7. H. Jagersma, *A History of Israel to Bar Kochba*, SCM Press 1994, vol. 1, p. 50.

8. A. J. Heschel, *The Sabbath*, Farrar, Straus & Giroux 1951, p. 50.

9. The famous hymn to Aten is included in the volume *Near Eastern Texts* mentioned in n. 2 above, pp. 369–71.

10. Sigmund Freud, *Moses and Monotheism*, Hogarth Press, 1939.

11. See R. H. Charles, *Eschatology*, Shocken Books 1963, pp. 301–3.

2. Zoroaster

1. For the Bisitun inscription, see Mary Boyce, *Textual Sources for the Study of Zoroastrianism*, University of Chicago Press 1984, p. 104. Ahura Mazda, 'Lord of Wisdom', was the Old Persian name for God in the earliest Zoroastrian texts. At a later time he was called Ohrmuzd, which is the Pahlavi form of the name. Similarly, Angra Mainyu, the Old Persian name for the 'Spirit of Evil', was later called Ahriman. Since in this book we are concerned with Zoroaster rather than with the religion which he generated, I have used the Old Persian names current in his time, though sometimes I may be referring to a later text. For the prophet himself, I have used the name Zoroaster, although this is a form of his name derived from Greek writers. The Old Persian form of the name was Zarathushtra. I think that Zoroaster is the form best-known to English speakers, and of course the religion derived from him is known as Zoroastrianism. The name Zarathustra is known in the West chiefly through Nietzsche's famous book, *Thus Spake Zarathustra*, but this is a very different Zarathustra from the original!
2. Ninian Smart, *The Religious Experience of Mankind*, Scribner 1969, p. 241.
3. See Boyce, op.cit., p. 108.
4. Ibid., p. 75.
5. Ibid., p. 76.
6. Ibid., p. 77.
7. Ibid., p. 57.
8. A. C. Bouquet, *Sacred Books of the World*, Penguin Books 1954, p. 111.
9. Boyce, op.cit., p. 35.
10. Ibid., p. 41.
11. Ibid., p. 42.
12. Charles Gore, *The Philosophy of the Good Life*, John Murray 1930, p. 52.

3. Lao-zu

1. For a summary of Si-ma Qien's account of Lao-zu and Juang-zu, see James Legge (ed.), *The Texts of Taoism*, vol. 1, pp. 33–38, Dover Publications 1962 (reprinted from the Oxford University

Press series, 'Sacred Books of the East,' 1891). Legge uses the older transliterations, Sse-ma Khien, Lao Tzu and Chuang Tzu.

2. Ibid., pp. 34–5.
3. Ibid., pp. 201–2.
4. Martin Palmer, *The Elements of Taoism*, Element Books 1991, p. 36.
5. Quotations from the *Tao Te Ching* are mainly from Legge's translation (see n. 1 above); sometimes from the translation by E. R. Hughes in *Chinese Philosophy in Classical Times*, Dent 1942.
6. See especially Heidegger's 'What Is Metaphysics?' in *Basic Writings*, Routledge 1977.
7. Chapter references for quotations from the *Tao Te Ching* are given in the text.
8. Quoted by Palmer, *Elements*, p. 60.
9. See Plotinus, *Enneads*, especially Book V, ed. A. H. Armstrong, Loeb Classical Library 1984.
10. John Macquarrie, *The Concept of Peace*, SCM Press 1973, p. 16.
11. Palmer, op.cit., pp. 13–19.
12. Juang-zu in Legge, vol. 1, p. 189.

4. *Buddha*

1. E. J. Thomas explains how this date is reached in his *The Life of Buddha as Legend and History*, Kegan Paul 1931, Routledge 1949, p. 27, n. 1.
2. Ibid., pp. 51–2.
3. The expression 'leave the world' means to take up the life of a religious ascetic.
4. Thomas, op.cit., p. 52.
5. 'There is nothing for me beyond this world': the words mean that he will not be reborn into the world.
6. Thomas, op.cit., p. 68.
7. Ibid., p. 87.
8. Ibid., pp. 87–8.
9. Christmas Humphreys, *The Wisdom of Buddhism*, Michael Joseph 1960, p. 56.
10. Ibid., pp. 65–70.
11. Quotations are from Max Müller's translation, included in his

book *The Science of Religion*, Scribner 1893, pp. 149–300.
12. See his essay, 'Buddhist Nihilism', ibid., pp. 129–47.
13. For the 'Buddha within,' see Humphreys, ibid., pp. 37–8. John Hick has some very clarifying discussions of the *Dharmakaya* and its relation to other ultimates in *An Interpretation of Religion*, Macmillan and Yale University Press 1989.

5. Confucius

1. *Analects*, 7.1. In quoting from *The Analects*, I have used D. C. Lau's translation, Penguin Books 1979. For a few passages, I have used E. R. Hughes, *Chinese Philosophy in Classical Times*, Dent 1942.
2. John Locke, *Of Civil Government* Dent 1924, pp. 119, 126.
3. *Analects*, 9.6.
4. Ibid., 2.4.
5. H. G. Creel, *Confucius and the Chinese Way*, Harper 1949, p. 169. I am indebted to this book for much of the biographical information about Confucius.
6. See above, p. 46.
7. Lau, op.cit., p. 12.
8. Mencius is the latinized form of the name Meng-zu.
9. *Analects*, 15.24.
10. Ibid., 4.4; 15.9; 4.5.
11. Ibid., 4.6.
12. Ibid., 7.34.
13. Ibid., 14.4.
14. Creel, op.cit., pp. 165–6.
15. *Analects*, 7.21.
16. Ibid., 11.12.
17. Ibid., 6.18.
18. Ibid., 15.31.
19. See above, p. 41.

6. Socrates

In the notes to this chapter, references to the writings of Plato are followed by page references to English translations. J indicates the standard translation by Benjamin Jowett, *Dialogues of Plato*, Random Press 1937, two volumes. L indicates the

translation of the three specifically Socratic dialogues by R. W.
Livingstone contained in his book *Portrait of Socrates*, Oxford
University Press 1938.

1. Cicero, *Treatises*, tr. C. D. Yonge, Bell 1871, p. 292.
2. Walter Burkert, *Greek Religion*, tr. John Raffan, Harvard
   University Press 1985, p. 305.
3. Justin Martyr, *Writings*, tr. T. B. Falls, Christian Heritage 1948,
   p. 83.
4. Xenophon, *Memorabilia* I, 1, 2, Loeb Classical Library 1923,
   p. 3.
5. See above, p. 9.
6. A. E. Taylor, *Socrates* Peter Davies 1935, p. 68ff.
7. Ibid., p. 16.
8. Ibid., pp. 37–8.
9. Plato, *Apology*, 31 (J I, 414; L 29).
10. Ibid., 21 (J I, 404; L 10).
11. Burkert, ibid., pp. 301–3. Cf. Taylor, pp. 148–9; Livingstone,
    pp. 82–83.
12. Plato, ibid., 38 (J I, 420; L 40).
13. Ibid., 35 (J I, 418; L 36).
14. Ibid., 36 (J I, 418; L 38).
15. Ibid., 29 (J I, 412; L 26).
16. See above, pp. 81–2.
17. Ibid., 40 (J I, 422; L 45–6).
18. Ibid., 42 (J I, 423; L 48).

7. *Krishna*

1. See Klaus Klostermaier, *Hindu and Christian in Vrindaban*,
   SCM Press and Westminster/John Knox Press 1969.
2. The *Mahabharata* is one of the two great Indian epics (the other
   being the *Ramayana*) and reached its present form about
   400 CE, though it contains much old traditional material.
   English versions (abridged) include one by William Buck
   (University of California Press 1973) and a shorter one by
   Shanta Ramashwar Rao (Disha Books 1992).
3. Paul Masson-Oursel *et al.*, *Ancient India*, Routledge 1934,
   p. 172.

4. The *Bhagavadgita* is part of the *Mahabharata* but is often published separately. I have used R. C. Zaehner's edition which contains a transliterated text, translation and commentary (Oxford University Press 1969).

5. Zaehner, op. cit., p. 177; cf. S. Radhakrishnan, *The Principal Upanishads*, George Allen & Unwin 1953, p. 643.

6. Ibid., p. 229.

7. See above, pp. 11–12.

8. E.g., St Thomas Aquinas.

9. Zaehner, op. cit., p. 184.

10. A. C. Bouquet, *Comparative Religion*, Penguin Books 1942, p. 137.

11. Zaehner, op.cit., p. 400.

12. Ibid., p. 398.

13. Ibid., p. 395.

14. Ibid., p. 133.

15. Ibid., p. 286.

16. Ibid., p. 400.

8. *Jesus*

1. The New Testament Chronological Table in *Das Grosse Bibellexikon*, Brockhaus 1987, vol. 1, pp. 242–3 gives the date 8/7 BCE. The accompanying article discusses various possibilities and assesses the evidence. Of course, it is generally acknowledged that the chronology of Jesus' life can be known only in a very approximate way.

2. I do not discuss here the tradition of a virginal conception. For an opinion on this topic, see my book *Jesus Christ in Modern Thought*, SCM Press and Trinity Press International, 1990, pp. 393–4.

3. Geza Vermes, *Jesus the Jew* (Collins 1973), SCM Press and Fortress Press 1994, p. 22.

4. C. Guignebert, *Jesus*, Kegan Paul 1935, p. 135.

5. Vermes, op.cit., p. 83.

6. W. D. Davies, *The Sermon on the Mount*, Cambridge University Press 1966, p. 31.

7. See A. E. Harvey, *Strenuous Commands*, SCM Press and Trinity Press International 1990.

8. See Macquarrie, op.cit., pp. 398–400.

9. See above, p. 106.
10. John Knox, *The Death of Christ*, Abingdon Press 1958, p. 84; E. P. Sanders, *Jesus and Judaism*, SCM Press and Fortress Press 1985, p. 305.
11. See above, pp. 19–20.
12. Further evidence that Jesus had friends in the city.
13. C. H. Dodd, *The Founder of Christianity*, Collins 1971, p. 26.
14. Tacitus, *Annales*, 15, 44. The passage is included in *A New Eusebius*, ed. J. Stevenson, rev. W. H. C. Frend, SPCK 1987, pp. 2–3.

9. Muhammad

1. Quoted by Kenneth Cragg, *The Call of the Minaret*, Orbis Books[2] 1985, p. 63.
2. *Koran* 96, 1–4. For quotatons from the *Koran*, I have generally used the translation by E. H. Palmer. This originally appeared as volumes 6 and 9 in the series 'Sacred Books of the East', edited by F. Max Müller. The whole work was reissued as a single volume, but preserving the original pagination. This is the edition which I have used. The translation by J. M. Rodwell has rearranged the suras of the *Koran* in what is believed to be their approximate chronological order. Further references to the *Koran* will be abbreviated to K., followed by the numbers of sura and verse.
3. K., 10, 73 and 84.
4. See above, p. 77.
5. K., 13, 29.
6. K., 17, 107.
7. See D. S. Margoliouth, *Mohammed and the Rise of Islam*, Putnam 1923, especially chapter 3, 'Islam as a Secret Society', pp. 83–117.
8. K., 72, 3.
9. K., 17, 2.
10. Margoliouth, op.cit., pp. 220–1.
11. Cragg, op.cit., p. 26.
12. Margoliouth, op.cit., p. 203.
13. K., 2, 214.
14. K., 33, 36.
15. K., 8, 9.

16. Cragg, op.cit., p. 32.
17. K., 112.
18. Quoted by C. R. North, *An Outline of Islam*, Epworth Press 1934, p. 108.
19. K., 16, 27.
20. Margoliouth, op.cit., p. 324.

Conclusion

1. See above, pp. 7–8.
2. See above, pp. 9–10.
3. The word 'supernatural' has various meanings. Here I intend what may be called the 'bad' meaning when events in this world that are not properly understood are ascribed to agencies beyond the world.
4. See above, p. 10.
5. *The Assumption of Moses* is a non-canonical writing which exists only in fragmentary form. An account of it is given in R. H. Charles, *Eschatology*, Schocken Books 1963, pp. 301–3.
6. See above, p. 80.
7. *Koran* 3, 45.
8. John Hick, *An Interpretation of Religion*, Macmillan and Yale University Press 1989, p. 10.
9. John Bowker, *The Religious Imagination and the Sense of God*, Oxford University Press, 1978, p. 260.
10. Xenophon, *Memorabilia*, I, 2,64.
11. *Bhagavadgita*, ch. 11.
12. Eckhart, *Sermons*, tr. R. B. Blakney, Harper 1957, p. 169.
13. Paul Tillich, *The Courage to Be*, Collins 1962, p. 176.
14. F. H. Bradley, *Appearance and Reality*, Oxford University Press 1893, pp. 470ff.
15. Karl Jaspers, *Philosophical Faith and Revelation*, Harper 1967, p. 144.
16. Athanasius, *De Incarnatione*, 41.
17. See above, p. 96.
18. A. J. Heschel, *The Prophets*, Harper 1962, p. 224.
19. J. Macquarrie, *Jesus Christ in Modern Thought*, SCM Press and Trinity Press International 1990, ch. 20.

Appendix

1. John Van Seters, *The Life of Moses: The Yahwist as Historian in Exodus-Numbers*, Westminster/John Knox Press Louisville 1994.
2. See above, p. 113.
3. Paul Meier, 'The Date of the Nativity and the Chronology of Jesus' Life', in *Chronos, Kairos, Christos*, ed. J. Vardaman and E. M. Yamauchi, Eisenbrauns, Winona Lake 1989.
4. N. Kokkinos, 'Crucifixion in AD 36', ibid.

Index